CONTENTS

POWER-SHARING ISLAM?

POWER-SHARING ISLAM?

Edited by

Azzam Tamimi

LIBERTY *for Muslim World* PUBLICATIONS

Power-sharing Islam?
Papers from the London one-day International Symposium organised jointly by Liberty, a London-based international organisation concerned with the defence of human rights and civil liberties and the promotion of democracy in the Muslim World, and by the Centre for the Study of Democracy at the University of Westminster

Sponsored by the University's Short Courses Unit, the symposium was held at the University of Westminster on 20 February 1993

ISBN: 0-9521672-0-4

The relevant CIP catalogue record for this book is available from the British Library

Printed in the United Kingdom

Enquiries:

Liberty
BM Freedom
London WC1N 3XX
U.K.

I INTRODUCTION

As the breeze of democracy blows over many parts of the third world, an increasing number of Muslim countries - since the mid-eighties - have been transforming their political systems in favour of democracy. However, the transition has not been easy. While in some countries democracy has reconciled historical foes, in other countries the process has resulted in severe crises. One thing is certain, though, and that is the fact that in every case the initial response of mainstream Islamic movements had been to welcome democratisation and to express their readiness to participate in elections and to accept their results.

Until elections were held in countries like Egypt, Tunisia, Jordan, Algeria, Kuwait, and most recently the Yemen, the phenomenon of Islamic resurgence continued to be viewed in the West as an intolerant fundamentalist movement seeking to seize power through militant endeavours in order to impose strict Islamic laws that did not - at least in the eyes of many Westerners - respect human rights, tolerate differences or recognise the 'other'.

Although in the West much of this perception of Islam has been the product of historic misconceptions and disinformation dating back to the 11th century Crusade, the anti-West, Khomeyni-led Iranian revolution of 1979 and the subsequent tension between the West on the one hand and Iran and Iranian-backed militants in Lebanon on the other created an optimum medium for the revival of fears, anxieties and hostilities. Very few people in the West were really interested in understanding the background of Iran's revolution. Not much was said about the fact that it was essentially a popular revolution to rid the country of a dictator who - thanks to the support of his Western allies - oppressed his nation and attempted to force his people to abandon their culture and traditional values.

Throughout the eighties, neither the public nor the media in the West had the time or perhaps the willingness to learn more about Islam, which was given extremely bad coverage which associated it with terrorist activities undertaken by isolated groups of desparate and frustrated individuals. Had the Shah of Iran been a just democratic ruler, none of this would have happened. Had the West not protected and supported despotism in Iran, the former oppressive regime would not - as a measure of radical reaction - have been replaced by another form of dictatorship that seeks to legitimise its theocratic despotism through the adoption of some anomalous interpretation of Islam.

It is now evident that in the cases where democracy was respected - such as in Jordan, Kuwait and the Yemen - the Islamists have been incorporated into the system and have played a constructive role through power-sharing. In the cases where the process was aborted - such as in Egypt, Tunisia and Algeria - the Islamists were victimised and forced to search for alternative, far from peaceful, methods in order to achieve the goals they were prevented from achieving through the ballot box. The most regrettable cases of all are those of Tunisia and Algeria, where the victors in democratically held elections were not only stripped of their successes but repressed, detained, and severely punished.

On the first anniversary of the coup which brought an abrupt end to the democratic process in Algeria, Liberty and the Centre for the Study of Democracy at the University of Westminster jointly organised an international symposium entitled "POWER-SHARING ISLAM?". Its objective was to focus on the power-sharing tendencies and experiences of Islamic movements and to study the theory of power-sharing from Islamic and Western perspectives.

In view of recent international developments and changes in the global balance of power, the phenomenon of Islamic political resurgence will assume a rather important role in future world politics and should therefore receive proper attention. This need is especially urgent considering that only recently has an increasing number of political thinkers been realising that Islam is still widely misunderstood and underestimated in the West. Misconceived ideas and distortions about the religion of Islam continue to prejudice large sections of Western public opinion as well as many political, academic and media circles against Muslims in general and against Islamists in particular.

A considerable proportion of Westerners' knowledge about Islam is based on simplistic comparisons with other religions, especially Christianity. In this way, Islam is mistakenly perceived as a set of rituals restricted to humans' relationship with their Creator. In fact, the Arabic word *'islam'* means submission or resignation, that is obedience to the will of God, and this submission is understood to encompass all aspects of life. This is the unanimously accepted interpretation of the purposes of Islam. However, there existed in the past and still exist today individuals or groups who may opt for an aberrant interpretation which focuses on the spiritual aspects of Islam and completely or partially neglects its worldly aspects.

The first perfect model of the Islamic society, during the lifetime of Prophet Muhammad, emphasised the idea that the religion of Islam contains two types of relations. The first is the spiritual relationship between humans and their Creator, and the second is the worldly relationship among humans themselves. Since its inception more than fourteen centuries ago, Islam considered government to be an essential element of its social system. It is, therefore, only natural to expect such a system to collapse if stripped of this important component.

Both in the Holy Qur'an and the authentic collections of the Prophet's traditions, one can see clear evidence of the development of a sophisticated administrative organisation of society soon after Hijrah (migration from Mecca to Medinah). Then, the Prophet had two roles: spiritual, in his capacity as the Prophet through whom Divine teachings were revealed to the humans, and political, in his capacity as head and leader of the community.

The Medinah community consisted of Muslims, Jews and Pagans, and although only Muslims were expected to recognise Muhammad's prophethood, his leadership had to be recognised by all those who agreed to be members of the community, irrespective of their belief. A constitution known as the Al-Madinah Document was drawn up by the Prophet in order to organise relations, allocate responsibilities and to protect rights. Contemporary Muslim political thinkers, such as Rachid Ghannouchi of Tunisia, believe that the Al-Madinah document was the first of its kind in history to recognise the right to citizenship and to lay the foundations for a pluralistic society. Ghannouchi and others, such as Malek Bennabi of Algeria, find genuine democratic values in the practices of the early Muslims.

Following the death of the Prophet, his spiritual role was concluded for good, whereas his political role was transferred to his 'elected' successors who were accountable to the community. Scholars, or the learned people of Islam, resumed the role of teaching, advising, admonishing and interpreting. In so doing, the scholars claimed no theological or religious superiority or power over the community because Islam has never recognised priesthood or any form or degree of Divine representation or proxy. Incidently, this is an important distinguishing criteria between the Sunni political thought and the Shi'ite Imami political thought.

However, less than half a century after the Prophet's death, a despotic form of government evolved. Tribal monarchy, which is alien to Islam, was reinstated and it influenced, rather negatively, the progress of Islamic political thought and the development of its political institutions. Nevertheless, throughout the history of the Muslims until the collapse of the Islamic Caliphate much of the Shari'ah (or the canonical law of Islam) continued to be implemented according the community its Islamic identity.

Many contemporary Islamic thinkers consider the collapse of the Islamic Caliphate to be the most catastrophic event in the entire history of the Muslims. Islam as a way of life was suspended and an organised effort to westernise the Muslims was made in various parts of the Muslim world by governments and elites that were imposed on the community as a product of the colonial era. This explains why Islamic resurgence movements throughout the Muslim world - since the turn of the century - have had explicit political agendas and political ambitions.

The objective of Islamic revival movements has been to reinstate the Islamic way of life understood not as an end in itself but as a means of guaranteeing salvation in the Hereafter. In so doing, these movements have had to confront the westernisation campaigns aimed at undermining Islamic culture and Islamic values. Perhaps this is one of the reasons why Islamic political groups have been branded as fundamentalists, or militants or radicals, and have been unjustifiably accused of intolerance. Consequently, not much sympathy has been felt for the victims of dictatorship in many parts of the Muslim world, such as Algeria, Tunisia, Egypt and Tajekistan, because the prime victims have usually been the Islamists themselves.

This book is a humble effort to present the reader with a comprehensive treatment of issues related to Islam's stand on power-sharing, pluralism and democracy, together with first hand insiders' accounts of practical power-sharing experiences. Hopefully, 'POWER-SHARING ISLAM?' will contribute to the ongoing effort to bring about an intellectual rapproachement between Islamic and Western thinkers, to eliminate misconceptions about Islam and Islamic movements, and to dispel the unwarranted fears by many people in the West about the phenomenon of Islamic resurgence.

The ideas expressed in the papers contributed to this publication express the opinions of their authors and do not necessarily represent the convictions of either Liberty or the Centre for the Study of Democracy.

I wish to express my sincerest gratitude to Professor John Keane for his valuable comments and assistance throughout the production stages of this book.

Thanks to all the men and women who contributed to or participated in the London symposium and to the staff of the Short Courses Unit at the University of Westminster, especially Ms. Morag Jordan, who greatly contributed to the success of the POWER-SHARING ISLAM? symposium.

Special thanks to the University of Westminster for sponsoring and hosting the symposium, which I hope will be the first in a series of intellectual and cultural functions aimed at consolidating the dialogue between Islam and the West and investigating the vital questions raised by the phenomenon of Islamic resurgence.

AZZAM TAMIMI
London, June 1993

POWER-SHARING ISLAM

THE WESTERN PERSPECTIVES

This chapter consists of three papers presented by three Western political thinkers.

In the first paper entitled "Power-Sharing Islam?", Professor John Keane enters into a political dialogue with Islamists. He questions the dogmatic attitude of many Westerners toward Islam and Muslims and discusses a number of historical misconceptions. He remarks that modern Western political thought on the whole has been hostile to Islam and concludes that a case of unfortunate, often cruel and bloody misunderstanding has marked the relations between Islam and the West. Discussing the principle of democratic power-sharing, Professor Keane raises questions about the capacity of some Islamists to deal with some potential dilemmas, to accept the norms and procedures of democracy, and to tolerate diversity and criticism of Islam itself.

In the second paper entitled "Marxism and Islam: Failure and Success", Professor Ernest Gellner analyses from a sociological perspective the factors that have led to the twentieth century failure of Marxism and contrasts them with the factors that have been responsible for the survival and success of Islam.

In the third paper entitled "Bilateral Radicalisation", Francois Burgat focuses on the attitude of regimes in the Arab World toward Islamic opponents and on the attitude of the West toward the conflict between despotic regimes and Islamic groups in the Arab world.

POWER-SHARING ISLAM?

John Keane

Although the collapse of the Soviet Union and super-power rivalry has produced new patterns of disorder and uncertainty in the field of international relations, one trend is strikingly clear: the global demise of communism is producing a new bogey, the demon of Islam, against which there are growing calls for a new political crusade. The trend dates from the Iranian Revolution of 1979. In that year, in an extraordinary feat of insurrectionary radicalism, Khomeyni and his supporters demonstrated the immense power of a minority tradition of Shi'ite thinking. This current of Islamic thinking rejected Sunni contractual theories and condemned as corrupt any government not ruled by the Imam, the Caliph Ali or his representatives. To the surprise of most observers Islam did the unthinkable. It showed that a late twentieth century tyrant, armed to the teeth and backed by western investors and governments, could be toppled by popular pressure, and that the new Islamic regime installed by such pressure could stand politically between the two superpowers without being committed to either.

The Western reaction was frosty and it led to the invention of a new epithet called "Islamic fundamentalism". This term was a child of the Western media, which since that time has normally given Islam bad coverage — thanks to language problems, the absence of developed news agencies with international networks, and inadequate or biased reporting by some of its reporters and analysts. Since the Iranian Revolution the epithet has been deployed not only to refer to the militant resistance of those Islamic groups and parties, especially the Shi'a, who strictly oppose the interventionist policies of the West in their lands, but as a catch-all term to refer to any and every believer in Islam. Admittedly, some governments and politicians ruling in the name of Islam are treated more politely. For example, the Saudi government, who are nominally Sunni Wahhabies, are usually not called 'fundamentalists' in the Western media, presumably because their strategic importance to the West in military and trade and investment terms qualifies them as 'moderates'. Convenient blindspots of this kind are nevertheless exceptional. Everywhere in the West there are strong indications that Islam is becoming a synonym for fundamentalism. To speak of fundamentalism is to speak of Islam; to mention Islam is to talk of fundamentalism. Islam becomes a threatening OTHER: intolerant, gun-wielding, hijacking, fanatical, veiled, patriarchal, wife-beating, moralising on such subjects as alcohol, gambling and blasphemy. The threat of the Other is seen to be real and growing — a deadly conspiracy against the civilised world confirmed by such events as the occupation of the American embassy by students in Tehran, the angry squads of Islamic vigilantes that currently roam its streets in search of offenders against the *Shari'ah*, by Saddam Hussain's bullying of tiny Kuwait, and Imam Khomeyni's sentence of death against Salman Rushdie.

Some have suggested that this imagery of Islam as a new global threat is traceable to the Israeli lobby in Western politics. I do not accept this counter-conspiracy theory, although it is of some significance that Israeli foreign policy is currently abandoning its old strategy of forging alliances with countries like Turkey and Iran and neighbouring non-Arab minorities like the Kurds, in favour of policies based on the strategic assumption, outlined recently by Israeli President Chaim Herzog, that Islamic fundamentalism is 'the greatest single danger to the free world today'. The fictionalising of 'Islamic fundamentalism' has other and deeper roots.

In the West the whole of modern political thought, with few exceptions, has been hostile to Islam. Let me mention Voltaire, the renowned eighteenth-century French champion of enlightened compromise among conflicting religions and sects. In his *Traité sur la tolerance* (1762) Voltaire launched a witty attack on intolerance and its 'law of persecution' ('the law of *tygers*: nay, it is even still more savage, for *tygers* destroy only for the sake of food, whereas we have butchered one another on account of a sentence or a paragraph'). And yet Voltaire's plea for tolerance was never extended to Islam. He considered Turks a curse on the earth and, especially towards the end of his life, he spoke only in favour of their extermination. He confessed to Catherine the Great that the sacking of the Ottoman Empire would enable him to die content, adding his one regret: "*Je voudrais avoir du moins contribué a vous tuer quelques Turcs.*"

The European tradition of intellectual hostility to Islam is alive and well, and during the past decade it has undoubtedly fed the new ideology of Islam-as-Fundamentalism. According to Elie Kedourie, who until his recent death was Britain's most prominent scholar of contemporary Islamic politics, the political history of the Muslim states in North Africa and the Middle East during the past two centuries has been the unhappy story of endless power struggles rooted ultimately in historical Islam, which, influenced by the Byzantine and ancient Iranian traditions in the territories it conquered, made passive obedience to those who exercised power a religious duty. The result was oriental despotism — a type of regime in which the monopoly of state power effectively determines who enjoys the fruits of labour, a system where economic power, properly speaking, is non-existent and property is permanently insecure. Kedourie was certain: 'democracy is quite alien to the mind-set of Islam'.

The current Western claustrophobia about 'Islamic fundamentalism' has been heightened by such conclusions. But there are in addition three related developments which arguably harden the sense of Islam as 'invasive' of the West. First is the post-World War Two transformation of Western European countries into multi-national and multi-faith societies by the largest single recorded wave of migration in human history. In Western Europe alone more than 20 million people have settled permanently during the past several decades. A significant proportion of them are Muslims and this is producing anxiety in some quarters that Islam resembles a cancer in our body politic. Pierre Lelouche, key adviser to Jacques Chirac, subtly adds to these anxieties in his new book *Le nouveau monde*. He warns France — a country in which three and a half million Muslims live — of the growing dangers of Islamic fundamentalism and dictatorship and North-South confrontation. Sometimes concern about Muslim immigration is expressed in language as blunt as that of the former Belgian interior minister and member of the European Parliament, Joseph Michel: "We run the risk of becoming like the Roman people, invaded by barbarian peoples such as Arabs, Moroccans, Yugoslavs and Turks, people who come from far afield and have nothing in common with our civilisation". It is probable that that kind of language oils street-level violence against Muslims — Turkish Germans are murdered in Moelln and Soligen, Moroccans beaten up in the back streets of Marseille, and (as Fred Halliday's *Arabs in Exile* documents) during the Kuwaiti crisis and subsequent war in the Gulf, British Yemenis were physically attacked, their cafés harassed, their community associations threatened.

The Gulf War has added to this sentiment of an 'invasion' of the West by Islam. Live, on television screens, millions witnessed the spectacle of military confrontation with a dictatorship speaking the language of Islam. It appeared as if the Islamic enemy were in the next room, grabbing oil wells, plotting their next move, firing off medium-range missiles in the direction of our friendly neighbours. I am aware of the hypocrisy of these images on both sides — the Iraqi regime is most certainly not modelled on the *Shari'ah* and before the war it was treated as a key ally of the West — but the net consequence of the globalised Western media account of the war was to reinforce the sense of the Other as bearing down upon us.

Finally, and most recently, there is the story of Bosnia-Herzegovina. There, in south-central Europe, a civilised parliamentary democratic government presided over by a Muslim has been crippled by armed gunmen hungry for territory. Europe and the world currently stands by twiddling its thumbs, appeasing genocide, reinforcing the suspicion that Western policy has something to do with the fact that the Muslims of Bosnia are viewed as uncivilised non-Europeans, as worthless invaders. Although their roots in the region are five centuries deep, these European Muslims are shot at, herded at gunpoint from their burning homes, summarily executed in nearby houses or marched in columns to railway sidings, past rotting corpses to concentration camps, where they are raped or castrated, then made to wait — like the Jews before them — with bulging eyes and lanternous faces, for the arrival of their own death. Then, for posterity's sake, many newspaper and television reports of the genocidal war offer their audiences a most curious sub-text: war and butchery of this kind is what we expect from the Balkans, which is not genuinely European, if only because Islam is at work there, right on our doorstep.

In the face of these overlapping trends some Islamists have attempted to combat the ideology of Islam-as-Fundamentalism by demonstrating Islam's capacity for power-sharing and, thus, its compatibility with the modern democratic West. There are those — the Egyptian writer Ahmad Shawqui al-Fanjari is among the boldest and most influential — who deduce every conceivable democratic right and duty from the Qur'an, the Traditions of the Prophet, and the practice of the first four Caliphs. Fanjari, following the example of Tahtawi, the famous pioneer of cultural westernisation in Egypt, says that every age adopts a different terminology to convey the concepts of democracy and freedom. What is called freedom in Europe is exactly what in Islam is called justice (*'adl*), truth (*haqq*), consultation (*Shura*) and equality (*Musawat*). Fanjari says " the equivalent of freedom in Islam is kindness or mercy (*rahmah*) and that of democracy is mutual kindness (*tarahum*)". He goes on to remind his readers that in the Qur'an the Prophet is instructed to show leniency and forgiveness in the very same verse as he is ordered to consult the believers in the affairs of the community. The Prophet is reported to have said in turn that God "has laid down consultation as a mercy for His community". It follows from this interpretation that, contrary to Kedourie and others, Islam is indeed compatible with democracy because there is no place in it for arbitrary rule by one man or group of men. The basis of all decisions and actions of an Islamic state should be not individual whim and caprice, but the *Shari'ah* - the body of regulations drawn from the Qur'an and the Traditions. Moreover, it is said that Islam passes another test of democracy, viz., the requirement that any government should reckon in all its decisions with the wishes of the ruled. In listing the qualities of a good believer the Qur'an mentions *shura* (consultation) and *ijima'* (consensus) on the same footing as compliance with God's order, saying the prayers and payment of the alms-tax.

This type of argument about the democratic potential of Islam, so eloquently formulated by Ahmad Shawqui al-Fanjari, deserves widespread attention. Both within the Islamic and Western worlds cosmopolitan Islam, as I would call it, is a potential force for mutual understanding and power-sharing, exactly because it challenges the dogma that the teachings of Islam are essentially fundamentalist. Many Western intellectuals and a large majority of Western citizens are simply unaware of the existence of cosmopolitan Islam. That is a pity because such ignorance serves to underpin the foundations of the ideology of anti-Islam, thereby making life more difficult for Islamists living in the West and Islamists making politics within states on the margins of the West.

Are we then to summarise the current impasse in relations between the Islamic and non-Islamic worlds in terms of an unfortunate misunderstanding? Is the priority in both worlds that of helping Islam escape the prison cell to which it has been assigned by Western journalists and politicians and Shi'ite fundamentalism? Yes. But in my view there are two other related issues that require urgent attention if Islam is to be seen widely as a force for power-sharing.

Especially in countries in which Islam is potentially a dominant social force, Islamic politics is faced by a strategic difficulty that I would call **the transition to democracy dilemma**. Any Islamic movement that attempts to transform a non-Islamic into an Islamic state is forced to choose between two incompatibles — principles and power. Islamic parties that are dedicated to parliamentary democracy do so on the assumption that their enemies are reasonable human beings, and this in turn limits their range of political tactics. They embrace public discussion, press conferences, vote-getting, and parliamentary numbers, rather than terrorism, street violence, and dreams of a revolutionary putsch. When elected to office it follows that those Islamic parties eschew dictatorship as a means of staying in office. If voted out of office, they then leave peacefully, to prepare for future electoral battles.

Of course an Islamic movement that remains faithful to its own principles and to these democratic procedures may never achieve governmental power. Especially in contexts where its opponents do not abide by the power-sharing rules of democracy, Islamists may find themselves outwitted, censored, beaten up, arrested, executed, or forced into exile. Under such circumstances, which are today the norm for most followers of Islam, does this mean that the vision of a democratic Islamic state is impossible? Or can an Islamic state be achieved only if Islamists are prepared to abandon the democratic method temporarily to attain power by violence in the pious hope that an Islamic government so formed will return to parliamentarism once Islam has assumed control? Needless to say, this second alternative contains tragic possibilities: a movement for democracy that resorts to despotic methods to achieve its goals will not remain a democratic movement for long. Its chosen means will devour its chosen ends. And yet — here is the painful dilemma — the first alternative, that of clinging to parliamentary democratic procedures under all circumstances, may well doom Islam to a permanent political wilderness.

The transition to democracy dilemma is real. A case in point is the current brutal treatment of Islamists by the military-dominated High Committee of State in Algeria, in whose first multi-party general elections in December 1991 the Front Islamique du Salut (FIS) won an absolute majority of votes. However, in the long run I do not think it is necessarily a cause for pessimism. While by definition a dilemma is insoluble, its force can in practice be attenuated, and I would therefore hope that Islamic political thinkers and actors will set their imaginations loose on the problem of how to maximise the chances of securing a democratic Islamic state in contexts where its bully opponents don't play by the rules of the democratic game. I cannot here provide detailed recommendations, but three points should be clear.

First, an Islamic party or government which comes to power and rules by terror, force, and intrigue is a contradiction in terms. It is (to resort to the arguments of Ahmad Shawqui al-Fanjari) anti-Islamic and therefore anti-democratic. Second, it should always be remembered that in the struggle for more democracy the methods used strongly condition the tactics and methods of its opponents. The latter are never simply given, and they should not be thought to be so. Successful transitions to democracy are always a learning process in which — the recent 'velvet revolutions' of central and eastern Europe are striking cases in point — opponents of democracy can sometimes be convinced to minimise their acts of sabotage and to relinquish at least some of their power democratically. The Jordanian government of King Hussein might be an example. The point is that terror breeds fear and armed *jihad* breeds military crackdown, while peaceful democratic methods can be infectious, if only because even their opponents can see that they enable everybody to sleep peacefully in their beds at night.

Finally, the political dilemma confronting contemporary Islamists who pursue the parliamentary road can be further weakened by their refusal to make a fetish of sovereign state power. For a variety of reasons we are witnessing a global decline of nation-state sovereignty. Our world is beginning to resemble the <u>form</u> of the mediaeval world, in which monarchs were forced to share power and authority with a variety of subordinate and higher powers. The trend has profound implications for the struggle for an Islamic state. It renders implausible the revolutionary strategy of seizing state power, if need be through the use of force, precisely because the 'centres' of state power are tending to become more dispersed and, hence, immune from 'capture' by a single party or government. Not only that, but insofar as 'the state' ceases to be in one place to be 'seized' the struggle by Islamists to monopolise state is rendered unnecessary. The often poorly coordinated and dispersed character of state power, whether in Egypt, Morocco, or Malaysia, makes it ever more susceptible to the initiatives of social organisations and movements which mobilise traditional 'folk' Islam and cultivate its 'grass-roots' networks, above all in local mosques, clinics and schools, to practise the art of divide-and-rule from below. In other words, Islam, the most socially conscious of world religions, can partly overcome the transition-to-democracy dilemma by concentrating the considerable sum of its energies on the nooks and crannies of civil society. There, in areas of life underneath and outside of the state, it can empower its followers by stimulating their awareness that large-scale organisations, such as state bureaucracies and trans-national firms, ultimately rest upon the molecular networks of power of civil society — and that the strengthening and transformation of these micro-power relations necessarily effects the operations of those large scale organisations.

The strategy of supplementing 'the parliamentary road to Islam' with the creation 'from below' of an Islamic movement rooted in civil society offers not only a practical way of moderating the transition-to-democracy dilemma. It clearly offers the hope of greater dignity to people who have been pauperised materially and spiritually by western or Soviet modernisation — people such as the poor of Cairo and the young people from quarters in Algiers like Bab al-Oued, where talk is now mainly about elusive visas and emigration, and memories of friends killed on the streets by the crack of army gun-fire. The strategy is however two-edged, for it contains another fundamental dilemma facing those who want to shatter the ideology of Islam-as-fundamentalism and who yearn for an Islamic state in which power is shared peacefully. I am referring to **the dilemma of pluralism**.

Nearly a third of the world's believers in Islam live in countries in which they can never hope to become a numerical majority of the population. In those countries, India for example, Islamists have no alternative but to espouse the cause of toleration and civil and political liberties for all. If they do not, then they weaken their own social and political credibility, especially in the eyes of a potentially threatening and threatened non-Islamic majority concerned about 'Islamic fundamentalism'. The point here is that the toleration of differences is not divisible. Those Islamists who claim recognition of their particular identity have a *tu quoque* obligation to recognise the particular identity of others. That recognition of heterogeneity in turn implies support for non-religious institutions — such as an independent judiciary and a pluralistic media — capable of protecting not only Hindus and Parsees, Jains and Sikhs, Christians and Jews, believers and non-believers, but also Islam itself. Living as a minority in the midst of a majority, Islam, paradoxically, is forced to acknowledge the limits of Islam as a religion claiming to be universal.

The same dilemma of pluralism is evident in countries, Pakistan and Iran for example, where Islam is a majority or near-majority religion and where the principles of Islam have been encoded in the dominant legal, political and social institutions. In such countries the toleration of non-Islamic ways of life 'outside' the Islamic community remains an important priority. Yet precisely because Islam is dominant there emerges the additional problem of whether and to what extent Islam tolerates forms of life and expression that are anathema to Islam. A different question — one that is always present but usually latent in non-Islamic countries — constantly surfaces within the community of Islamic believers itself: To what extent can and should Islam, if only for the sake of its power-sharing image, sanction the birth of pluralism within its own body politic by tolerating competing interpretations of Islam by Islamists themselves, especially interpretations which say the unsayable or announce to their fellow-Muslims things that are either incomprehensible or inconceivable or objectionable?

The history of world religions suggests that no religion can painlessly tolerate heretics within its own ranks, and it is therefore not surprising that contemporary Islamic regimes have reacted in various and conflicting ways to pluralising trends. Two contrary examples — from Pakistan and Iran — spring to mind.

The fate of the Urdu writer Mumtaz Mufti's *Labbaik,* a satirical account of his pilgrimage to Mecca, serves as a reminder that Islam contains rich traditions of internal dissent — and that the ideology of Islam-as-Fundamentalism is itself a concocted dogma. First published in Pakistan in 1975, *Labbaik* is written as a pilgrimage (*hajj*) narrative riddled with irony, disjunction, and daring similes. On the PIA flight from Karachi to Jeddah, Mufti sits in economy class, among the pious and solemn-faced pilgrims, telling their beads. In first class, the Pakistan hockey team, off to a match, periodically explodes in rollicking laughter. The hockey players, Mufti suggests, are hijackers whose laughter expresses their power over the hijacked, the pilgrims. In Jeddah Mufti lodges in an absurdly luxurious hotel with every Western-style amenity, fantasising his room as a 'honeymoon suite'. He again chooses five-star luxury in Mecca, imagining himself among relics of the Raj, including the old mem of the hotel, who sits on his lap and says (in English), 'Darling, don't be so superstitious.' Within the sanctuary in Mecca he more or less sees Allah, before whom he confesses himself to be merely a self-centred Hindu idol. Throughout his stay he carefully observes how his fellow pilgrims treat the *hajj* as a dry-cleaning factory in the business of removing sins or as a booking-office for journeys to paradise. Mufti also shows up the impracticalities of their other-worldliness: 'My sincere advice when you go on *hajj* is that you take along a good pair of scissors'.

Coming from the hand of one of the most prominent Urdu novelists, *Labbaik* generated considerable controversy in Pakistan. The author made it clear that his contempt for the clerics of Islam was linked to his attempt to locate himself personally within the Islamic tradition into which he was born. Displaying a Sufi skepticism towards formal religion and a healthy mockery of his own imitation of the West, Mufti held firm to a conclusion in which generations of Westernised Muslims have sought refuge: that at the very least Mecca belongs even to those whose faith is halting and occasional and that despite their doubts they respect the Prophet Muhammad as 'a great man'. *Labbaik* was frequently condemned as blasphemous, and there were certainly attempts to ban it. Yet there were those, up-ending the meaning of the term, who insisted that it would be *kufr*, or infidelity, to condemn a book of such great artistic merit. The matter was resolved when the then Minister of Religious Affairs, himself a sometime member of the Jama'at party and also a literary figure, wrote a preface for the second edition in which he predicted that the pilgrimage account would earn the author a place in paradise.

Such official courting of pluralist dissent within Islam contrasts strikingly with the repressive anti-secularism of the Iranian regime. During the past year sixty Iranian intellectuals, including writers and journalists, have signed a petition condemning the continuing *fatwa* against British novelist Salman Rushdie. The petition has been dealt a harsh blow by the Iranian government, which has officially banned the works of all the signatories, including the poets Esmail Kho'i and Nader Naderpour. This reaction ought to be of interest not because it highlights the continuing despotism of the Iranian regime but because it demonstrates a different — ideological — way of dealing with the dilemma of pluralism confronting the Islamic tradition. Salman Rushdie's *The Satanic Verses* has indeed caused widespread offence to many followers of Islam — most of whom have never read it — and this has prompted widespread calls for its banning and burning and, especially in Iranian government circles, Rushdie's death. The anti-secularists in that country have particularly emphasised Rushdie's doubting of the authenticity of the revelations recorded in the Qur'an. In two complex chapters reporting a dream of one of the central characters of *The Satanic Verses,* Rushdie explores the birth and triumph of Islam. In its attempts to outmanoeuvre the old pre-Islamic world, Rushdie writes, Islam was inevitably faced with numerous dilemmas and compromises, which he highlights, Mahound (that is, Muhammed) is described as a 'Businessman' constantly doing deals with the archangel and God, who is also 'really a Businessman' who offers the Prophet good deals and bargains and helps in sticky situations. Muhammed is also called a 'smart bastard' who lays down rules that suit him. He is pictured as a lustful philanderer who slept with so many women within a year after his wife's death that his beard turned 'half-white'. And the Qur'an is mocked as a book 'spouting' rules about how to 'clean one's behind', 'fart' and to engage in sexual intercourse, including sodomy.

Islamist critics of profanity have attacked these literary similes in several ways. Some have objected to their 'scurrilous' and 'abusive' transgression of *hodud* (the ethical limits of decency) and to their reinforcement of the ideology of Islam-as-Fundamentalism; others to their wholly 'untruthful' historical account of the rise of Islam; and still others have insisted that Rushdie is guilty of *ridda* (apostasy), in the sense that he has violated solemn commitments and treacherously 'turned back' on Islam, forsaking it for unbelief or another religion. Considered together, these accusations of perfidy are not *per se* inconsistent with democratic power-sharing. After all, democracies are systems of power in which opinions are sometimes publicly criticised as perfidious and things are called scandalous and in need of restriction or outright banning. Democracies require rules governing libel, defamation, and abuse. Yet — the qualification is important — the long-term political designs lurking behind the calls for censorship and punishment of the author of *The Satanic Verses* are different in kind, exactly because their anti-pluralism is inconsistent with democracy, minimally defined.

In contrast to all forms of authoritarian government, democracy comprises procedures for arriving at collective decisions through public controversies and compromises based on the fullest possible participation of citizens. At a minimum, democratic procedures include equal and universal adult suffrage within constituencies of various scope and size; and majority rule and guarantees of minority rights, which ensure that collective decisions are approved by a substantial number of those expected to make them. Democratic procedures also include freedom from arbitrary arrest and respect for the rule of law among citizens and their representatives; constitutional guarantees of freedom of assembly and expression and other civil and political liberties, which help guarantee that those expected to decide, or to elect those who decide, can choose from among real alternatives; and various social policies (in fields such as health, education, child care and basic income provision) which prevent market exchanges from becoming dominant and thereby ensure that citizens can live as free equals by enjoying basic political and civil entitlements. Expressed differently, democracy requires the institutional division between a certain form of state and civil society. A democracy is a system of open-ended institutions in which the exercise of power is flexibly controlled. It is a multi-layered political and social mosaic in which political decision-makers at the local, regional, national and supranational levels are assigned the job of serving the *res publica*, while, for their part, citizens living within the nooks and crannies of civil society are obliged to exercise vigilance in preventing each other and their rulers from abusing their powers and violating the spirit of the commonwealth.

Elsewhere (in *Democracy and Civil Society* [1988] and *The Media and Democracy* [1991]) I have argued at length that this minimum definition of democratic procedures is not wedded to any particular form of life and that, indeed, it is a basic precondition of the peaceful cohabitation of different forms of life in any given geographic area. So understood, democracy is not another ideology — by which I mean a moralising and power-hungry way of life claiming to be universal — but a condition of freedom from ideology. It is, in other words, the means by which a plurality of groups with different and often conflicting beliefs can live their differences and get along without murdering or dominating each other. Democracy institutionalises the right to be different. Democrats are not afraid that the intermingling of different groups and institutions will inevitably weaken or ruin democracy. Like Thomas Jefferson, who once remarked that 'it does me no injury for my neighbour to say that there are twenty Gods or no God', democrats champion tolerance and diversity. They are for freedom of religion as much as for freedom from religion. Democrats are pluralists. They celebrate hybridity and intermingling, and welcome the transformations that result from the combination of the new and the unexpected with the old and predictable. Democracy rejoices in hotchpotch, melange, and controversy, for that is how novelty enters the world. Democracy loves indeterminacy and change-by-conflict-and-compromise. It fears and resists the absolutism of the Pure, the Grand Ideology.

Defined in an ideological way, Islam potentially clashes with this basic feature of democracy because Islam itself is a special type of religion. Every religion is a system of beliefs based upon a minimum core of immutable and unquestionable tenets, which are held and practised on the strength of received conventions and traditional authority. Religion by definition has a dogmatic core and it is therefore on tense terms with democracy, which encourages ceaseless debate and self-questioning and, thus, public spaces for citizens to challenge and to reject many a sacred axiom. Democracy promotes secularism. Yet — it might be observed — Christianity and democracy proved to be compatible inasmuch as Western representative democracy as we know it has some Christian roots; various Christian sects previously at war with each other have also managed through the past several centuries to compromise peacefully, to agree the need for secular institutions, and to provide support for democracy. It may also be true, as Ali Kazancigil has suggested recently, that the present renaissance of Islam as a proselytising religion will be comparatively short-lived after it is forced to deal with the practical matters of economic development, social policy and government administration, that is, that in government Islam will lose its political aura and pave the way for its own 'secularisation', just as Christianity and other religions have done before it.

That is speculation. For the moment there remains a profound tension between democratic pluralism and dogmatic forms of Islam because Islam is a special form of religion that presents itself as a totality or complete way of life, not separable into the components to which we are accustomed in modern Western thought. The division of the world into sacred and profane, religious and secular, priesthood and laity does not exist in Islam. The separation of politics and ethics, politics and economics, church and state, state and civil society do not come naturally to it. Islam is a total life system — the Islamic *ummah,* the community of the faithful who serve their sovereign God, provides guidance for the whole conduct of any individual or group. That is why, according to many Islamists, Salman Rushdie's *The Satanic Verses* is pernicious. It casts doubt upon the authenticity of the revelations recorded in the Qur'an and hence strikes at the heart of the whole Islamic code. Its circulation must therefore be prevented. Power-sharing with apostate secularists is wicked.

For genunie democrats this reasoning smacks of 'fundamentalism'. For them, not only does it fail to appreciate the ways in which *The Satanic Verses* is a deliberately polysemic work of literary fantasy. It also ignores the rights of the faithless and those who subscribe to non-Islamic faiths in a multi-faith era. It tacitly privileges Islam, doing so through the spurious argument that since people's beliefs, particularly their religious beliefs, are essential to their self-identity, any attack on their beliefs is equivalent to assaulting persons. That conclusion, democrats say, is absurd. It amounts to the dogmatic principle that each individual, group, or religion is entitled to veto public criticism of whatever beliefs they deem central to their own particular identity.

The bitter disagreements displayed in the Rushdie affair highlight the dilemma of pluralism facing Islamists of all descriptions. Like the transition-to-democracy dilemma, it is probably insoluble, but that does not mean that ways cannot be found to effect ongoing working compromises. Democracies, ideally, are systems of complex liberty in which clashing entitlements and jurisdictional disputes are a permanent and legitimate feature of social and political life. Such openness is all too rare in relations between the West and Islam and it is obvious that the ideology of Islam-as-Fundamentalism is making things much more difficult than they need be.

There are certainly misunderstandings on both sides. I began by highlighting the Western media view that Islam is a religion of intolerance, misogyny, cruelty and political anarchy. But there are also profound suspicions on the Islamic side. Sometimes the contradictions of the West are grist to the mill of Islamists openly hostile to the West. Western double-standards are their favourite target. 'The West talks much about human rights, democracy and the need to protect minorities, but look at the reality of Western policy towards the Palestinians or the Bosnians or Tajikistan', it is said. 'We see hypocrisy rooted in a promiscuous and permissive society, a society marked by the decline of ethics, their replacement by money, weapons sales, hotel complexes, decadent consumerism and speeches by the Pope excusing rape'. I am trying hard not to exaggerate. Listen to the recent conclusion drawn by the 30-year old commander-in-chief of the Bosnian armed forces, Commander Zulfikar, himself a Muslim: "If you ask me the whole of the Western international community are bastards. Nobody is helping us. What's more, they have sold out and are accomplices to the extermination of our people and their own European culture."

The bitterness expressed by Zulfikar is warranted. It should disturb the dreams of all Western democrats. The violent destruction of the short-lived Bosnian experiment is a tragedy for many reasons, including the fact that it has deprived the world of a badly needed working model of an Islamic political community which practices democratic power-sharing. Arguably, the existence of such models would make the world a safer place by helping to undermine the ideology of Islam-as-Fundamentalism and to discharge the international and domestic tensions it is currently inciting. For the time being the friends of power-sharing must resort to chipping away at hypocrisy and power-mongering wherever it appears, buoyed by the thought that more democracy in both the Islamic and non-Islamic worlds might greatly help their mutual understanding and reconciliation — not because democracy is a panacea, which it is not, but because democracy is the enemy of enforced stereotyping, the most effective human weapon yet invented for dealing with arrogant armies, pompous politicians and power-hungry groups armed with ideologies.

MARXISM AND ISLAM: FAILURE AND SUCCESS

Ernest Gellner

There are two big events of this century which obviously deserve our attention. One is the failure of Marxism; the other is the success of Islam. I am an outsider to both these faiths. The terms I use are analytical or sociological. They do not imply endorsement or condemnation from an absolute viewpoint; they express the judgments of an observer of society concerned sympathetically with the fate of the people involved in these systems.

Let me begin with the failure of Marxism and my attempt to understand it. Marxism has often been compared, I think correctly, to a religion. It has many of the features of the advanced kind of religion which Professor Keane mentioned, although I think he was slightly narrow in highlighting religions which are centred on belief and doctrine and in rather underplaying the different kind of religion which is primarily ritualistic and traditional and non-doctrinal. Marxism had many of the features of a religion. It offered a total vision of the universe and of society and a combined vision of the two, so that social order and social righteousness were seen as corollaries of the total vision. In brief, it offered a path of salvation to mankind. It was unusual amongst religions in that it claimed to be entirely secular and this-worldly. It had no recognition of the transcendent, in fact it denied the transcendent, and I think what was fatal to it was that it had no division of the sacred and the profane. Paradoxically, it was a secular religion.

However, as we have learned in the last few years, it failed to resemble religions in one very important way — it had no great hold over the human heart. When other belief systems suffer a political defeat for better or for worse they retain a hold over the hearts of at least some of their adherents. People who have seen the world through the eyes of a certain vision, who were brought up in that vision, who identified the terms of that vision with their evaluation of their surroundings, are not easily weaned from it. Religion is like love, you cannot break it off overnight. It tends to go on tormenting you even if circumstances have frustrated it.

Something weird has happened in the case of Marxism. On my count in what could be called the previous Moscow zone, i.e. areas which were once under the influence of Moscow-based Marxism, there are now 29 separate countries: 15 in the Soviet Union, 5 in Yugoslavia and the rest in various parts of other Eastern European countries.

Whilst there are people hankering for the past because it was stable, there seems to be nobody hankering after the faith. When I say nobody I mean virtually nobody — there is no nostalgia. Somehow or other, Marxism has failed to do what other religions have succeeded in doing. Why is this? Of course the answer to this question like the answer to most questions is: I do not know. However I am going to offer you an hypothesis which explains Marxism's remarkable lack of magnetism.

Marxism is deeply pantheistic. Under pantheism there is a firm conviction of a single world: everything is one great unity and when salvation comes — and Marxism promised salvation — it will be pervasive and total. It is often said that man cannot live without religion. This may or may not be true, but it is conventionally asserted and has a certain plausibility.

I am offering you an alternative and less conventional suggestion, that men and societies cannot live without profanity. There has to be some part of the social world which is not sacred. This was the suggestion of the great sociologist Durkheim, when he considered the division of life into the sacred and the profane. He hit upon the very important truth that neither element is dispensable.

The intellectual origins of Marxism can be schematised very briefly by referring to Spinoza, Hegel and Marx. Spinoza was the greatest pantheist, who described how God-intoxicated man firmly abolished the division, and how the whole world was equally sacred, and had one pervasive deity — the pantheist vision. Hegel historicised this notion after taking it over, but saw this one great unity as manifesting itself in world history. Marx in turn took this over and endowed it with a materialist and economic content. At this time Russia and much of Eastern Europe were caught up in the struggle for equality and the emergence from underdevelopment, and it provided them with a vision which at one time seemed to work and which held the promise of catching up, of overtaking and of fulfilment.

In my reading of Soviet history I am struck by the strange fact that the unspeakable horror of the Stalin period did not erode faith in the religion. For instance, I studied with some care the memoirs of Andrei Sakharov, one of the finest minds of the century. They are very illuminating because Sakharov continued to be a believer in the overall vision, despite the fact that he despised all its individual propositions. Here we can see the total transformation of the human condition taking place. It is inevitably bloody and brutal and in working for it one might be justified in doing what Sakharov in fact did, namely equipping the Soviet Union with the H-bomb using slave labour and suppression.

In due course Sakharov was converted to a kind of dissidence both by the injustices of Soviet life and by the violation of scientific integrity. Lysenkoism was the major factor in his conversion, but the interesting fact is that he was never converted completely. Of course he knew with great intimacy all the horrors of the period. What did convert the citizens of the Soviet Union away from it was not the terror of Stalinism, but the squalor and inefficiency of the Brezhnev period. As long as they murdered each other, this was acceptable. When they started bribing each other it was not. Why not? Why should relatively minor sins, which are the common currency of most societies, be so profoundly unacceptable?

The answer I am suggesting to you is that Marxism, by sacralising the whole of social life, including the economic — by making the economic the sacrament of social righteousness — made squalor deeply corrosive. So, when the lid was finally taken off in the Gorbachev period, every one discovered with pleasurable surprise that the emperor was naked and that everybody else was naked as well. The faith which had survived random horrific murders and terror on a massive scale did not survive the truth about economic life, precisely because economic life was sacralised. Hence Marxism, while resembling religion in other ways, failed to have that tenacious hold over the human heart which other religions have.

Now let me consider the other major interesting phenomenon of our age, the victory and success of Islam. In the social sciences, one of the commonest theses is the secularisation thesis, which runs as follows. Under conditions prevailing in industrial-scientific society, the hold of religion over society and its people diminishes. By and large this is true, but it is not completely true, for there is one major exception — **Islam**. In the last hundred years the hold of Islam over Muslims has not diminished but has rather increased. It is one striking counter-example to the secularisation thesis. Like the failure of Marxism, it is a fascinating intellectual problem that serves as a background to the more practical, moral and political problems which are the concerns of this symposium.

I would tentatively and in all humility attempt to offer you an explanation. The Western perception of the strength of Islam is distorted by the fact that the West has largely noticed this fact in connection with the Khomeyni revolution. Although the Iranian revolution is, unquestionably, the most dramatic manifestation of the social and political vigour of Islam, it is in some interesting ways untypical, which somewhat distorts the perception. The social and political vigour of Islam is something which long antedates that particular revolution and ought not to be identified with it.

What is the sociological explanation of this counter-trend? I would suggest that two things need to be considered — the nature of high religions and the crisis of underdevelopment. Let me begin with the second.

Underdevelopment is the condition of a society which endures political humiliation as a result of a technological, and hence economic and military, inferiority. The uneven distribution of the benefits, if such they are, of modern technology in production and military hardware, has led to a curious kind of imbalance over the last two centuries, in which the early beneficiaries of technological power had their relative power enormously increased, and the later beneficiaries of course were temporarily disadvantaged. This is a key characteristic of the last two centuries. What is the characteristic reaction of a society to underdevelopment?

I think the paradigm of the reaction is the tension between Westernisation and populism. Many European countries have gone through this reaction, but it finds its supreme expression in the Russian literature of the 19th century. There are two ways that this reaction can be expressed. You can say, "Well, those Western bastards are very strong and powerful, we've got to pinch their fire, we've got to turn their weapons against them." Then of course you try to identify what the secret of their power is. Is it constitutionalism? Is it democracy? Is it science? The details of the diagnosis vary, but the outcome is that you try to redress the balance by emulating your enemy. A sensible strategy, but with one psychic disadvantage — the repudiation of your own local tradition, which is psychologically painful. It is not easy to say, "What our fathers and grandfathers did was deeply mistaken." Some Westernisers bring themselves to do it, but it is nevertheless painful.

The alternative is to say, "Not only are those Westerners bastards, but virtue is on our side." If you cannot idealise the government, which is usually difficult to do because they are caught between traditionalism and compromise with the past, you idealise some kind of local folk culture.

In the case of Russians of course it was the idealisation of the simple peasant soul. The simple peasant faith was seen to contain great virtue which compensated for its possible technological ineptness. Of course one can see with hindsight why Marxism was so tempting for Eastern Europe and for Russians because it did both things at the same time. It combined total mysticism and idealisation of the ultimate virtue in the human essence, with a promise not only to emulate the West but to overtake it without the weaknesses which were going to bring the West down. It was a deadly combination, and it was no doubt attractive. Yet in the end it proved disastrous, not only for the reasons I stated, but because its recipes for social organisation were incompatible with the preconditions for efficiency in the fourth or fifth industrial revolution, in an age of very rapid technological advance and computerisation.

That is my general analysis of the dilemma of underdevelopment which the entire world went through. You can include the French Enlightenment in the underdevelopment crisis. What the thinkers of the French Enlightenment were thinking is, "Why do those bastards, that nation of shop-keepers across the Channel, keep beating us ?" The answer was, "They've got some secret about social organisation which has escaped the French." So, although the notion of underdevelopment did not then exist, it really was the same kind of situation.

What then is the distinctive feature of Islam amongst the high religions? I think all high religions — by a high religion I mean a religion equipped with a scripture, a doctrine, and a professional core of interpreters — tend to suffer from a tension between the high variant and the folk variant. This takes a very specific form in Islam. The high variant is the faith of the scholars, unitarian, pure and puritan, spiritualist, anti-mediationist and anti-hierarchical. Their's is an egalitarian religion stressing the unity of God, the symmetry in the relationship between believer and God, with an ethic of rule observance rather than an ethic of loyalty to particular individuals. There is such a strong distrust of mediation, that there is a special name for the sin of associationship and of the use of mediators. By contrast, folk religion is more oriented towards mystical practices, hierarchy and a kind of surrogate priesthood in the form of cultish living saints.

If I read Muslim history correctly, within the history of Islam — from whenever it shook down after the early first centuries under the impact of the West — there was a tension between these two. Sometimes they lived in harmony, interpenetrating each other. Often the tension was expressed in the form of revivalist movements attempting to establish the true faith of the scholars against the corrupt version of the folk. Then came the impact of the West. Of course this occurred at different times and in different regions, as early as the Napoleonic invasion in Egypt, as late as the French invasion of Morocco in 1912, and even later in places like the Yemen.

Under the impact of Westernisation, Muslim society can reform itself without facing the dilemma which the Europeans faced, namely either to westernise or to idealise the folk culture. This is because it can invoke its own high tradition which is always respected, but usually not fully implemented — honoured in the breach, but not always in the observance. Muslims like to think that the high tradition goes back to the Prophet and his companions. I find this historically implausible, because I think that the circumstances in which they worked were different. But what is unquestionably true is that there is a genuine well-established old local tradition, and that it has many of the features which make it suitable for conferring what you may call international dignity: a very low level of magic, low ritualisation, egalitarianism and all kinds of features which make it compatible with modern conditions, and in particular the conditions of self-correction and industrial, economic and scientific catching up. Islam is more compatible with this than are the more hierarchical, ritual-ridden aspects of other religions. In brief, the Islamic World escapes the dilemma which, in my argument, pervades other societies caught in the trap of temporary underdevelopment.

Islam revives in the name of its own high tradition, not in the name of either the West or in the name of a populist idealisation of the folk culture. Muslims leave the latter to Western romantics; they do not themselves practise this and what they idealise is the old high tradition, in which case it appears as fundamentalism.

The definition of the term "fundamentalism" has a double edge, a double frontier. What fundamentalism says is that religion, its doctrines and its prescriptions are to be taken seriously; they mean what they say, neither more nor less. The doctrine of firm interpretation has of course two negations.

The first is a Western one which says that religion does not really mean what it says, and is in fact just a kind of symbolic expression. Talking to uneducated people like peasants and fishermen in Galilee, the founder of the dominant Western faith had to use simple language because if he talked modern philosophy they would not have understood him. But he really meant the latest philosophic fashion. So you get Christianity which in this sense tends to be vulgarised. In each generation it gets restated, and the basic message is: the doctrine does not mean what it says, it really means what the latest prophet has been saying, in simple language so that a simple fisherman can understand it.

The other one of course is esotericism: the doctrine of the hidden meaning, that there is a special secret way that the religion is stratified. Islamic fundamentalism fought on both these fronts. On the one hand, it opposed that alliance between itself and its folk use of mediators, while on the other hand it enhanced the stratification of an inner truth and an outer truth. If my diagnosis is correct, that the strength of Islam comes from this fundamentalism and self-correction in terms of a literal doctrine taken seriously, a kind of combination of simple and elegant unitarianism in theology with a firm set of rules for social life — why should the most dramatic manifestation of fundamentalism have appeared in Iran? It seems to go against the thesis, because of the sects established by the fissions in the early history of Islam, Shi'ism is of course in theological terms, furthest to the right, most given to a cult of personality, and to ritualism.

My answer to this is that although the cult of personality, combined with the cult of martyrdom, was very useful in the act of political mobilisation practised by Khomeyni, it was rapidly dropped in the course of success. What Khomeyni in fact did was Sunnify Islam. I have studied Khomeyni's works in the translation of his Welsh convert and acolyte Algar, and it seems to me very clear that the social and political doctrine of the kind of Islamic republicanism you get in Khomeyni's thought is a shift from a cult of personality to a cult of law, in other words a shift towards Sunnism.

Khomeyni does not deny the authority of the hidden Imams, but politically speaking he pensions them off. They are really politically irrelevant. What matters about religion is the implementation of the law. When the Imam comes back, of course, the authority will be his and he will take on government, but until he comes back the law must be implemented by those most competent to do so. Who else can do this but the lawyers? They will implement the law neither more nor less severely before or after his coming. His coming is almost a political accident. Khomeyni has rude things to say about such things as the cult of saints. So without actually abolishing the cult of personality there has been a kind of transfer or movement to a cult of the law away from the cult of personality, which I took to be the crucial distinguishing line between Sunnism and Shi'ism.

Let me now come back to the contrast with Marxism. Once again I have an interesting little disagreement — it is a matter of stress really — with Professor Keane. Professor Keane rightly pointed out that Islam is not just faith; it is an ordering of social life. Yes indeed, but it is an ordering of social life that does not fully sacralise it. In the regulation of economic life, for instance, Islam provides a set of hand rails so that people know where they are but it does not actually say that economic life in itself is sacred.

In other words, Muslims have a sphere of the profane to which they can retreat at times of less and maximum religious zeal. When it had the opportunity to play at the world of religion, Marxism deprived humanity of that zone precisely by sacralising the economic. If it had ritual and symbolic objects, they were the tractors, the images of muscular workers, huge socialist dams and so on. Economic life provided the sacraments for that religion. But when economic life in the end turned out to be both squalid and markedly less efficient, then Marxism collapsed. I think one of the most important factors in the final self-destruction of the Soviet Union was the discovery that Western capitalism could indeed be overtaken, but not by them; the people who were doing it were the Confucianists of East Asia and not the Marxists of the Euro-Asian centre. That discovery was crucial in causing the loss of faith which led to the self-dismantling of a system which had not provided a zone in which people could retreat when they wanted to work out their way.

Islam does provide for such a zone, which is one of the things which makes it a workable modern religion. It combines firm guidance in an idiom compatible with modern backgrounds, with a respect for the type of social division which is essential for a viable society.

BILATERAL RADICALISATION*

Francois Burgat

By virtue of an old political principle, regimes often have the opponents they deserve. Frequently their successors are the political forces which they themselves have largely helped to create.

If it were necessary to hold to this view in order to evoke the near future, pessimism would win out. In the spring of 1993, there is nothing that leads one to think that the misunderstandings linked to the rise in power of the Islamist challengers of the regime in place are likely to be overcome any time soon. None of the local situations, especially in Algeria, provides cause for much optimism.

A Bilateral Radicalisation

To the entire Arab political landscape, the 1991 parliamentary elections in Algeria have in fact transmitted a double message. Firstly, to the regimes, they have confirmed that no parliamentary elections would protect them from being defeated by their Islamist opponents as the ability of the supposedly 'small radical groups' to mobilise wider compartments of the society was clearly established. Most regimes have therefore both strengthened the prohibition made to the Islamist to accede to the institutional system and intensified a very 'preventive' repression against them. This has sometimes occurred (as in the case of Tunisia, Algeria and Egypt) without much regard for human rights.

Secondly, to the Islamist troops the way the results of the elections have been dismissed has underlined the poor credibility of the democratic discourse held both by the regimes and their foreign supporters. Inside the movements, it has therefore given more power to the backers of radicalisation.

While Algeria had at one time boasted of being the first Arab country to have a Minister of Human Rights (Ali Haroun, a member of the High State Committee), repression soon became the unique language of communication between the government and the duly elected representatives of the majority of the society. The detention camps have harboured as many as ten thousand militants whom the Algerian generals decided to extract by force from the political landscape, and whom they still hope to separate from the 3.5 million voters who have cast ballots in their favour during two elections.

Although it has not let the Ennahda movement demonstrate the width of its popular support, Tunis has also played the same repression-game with its opponents. In a country where, eleven years after the so called 'political opening' by former president Bourguiba, not one single seat has been gained by any of the opposition parties, Islamist or secularist — the 'defence of democracy' nevertheless still provides President Zine Al Abidine Ben Ali's regime with almost unlimited support from its western allies.

In Egypt, the already high level of violence increased during the summer of 1992. Some members of the Gemaa Islamiyya started assaulting foreign visitors, killing one British tourist and wounding three, in an attempt to force the regime to reduce the repression against its militants by depriving it of its valuable tourist income. The only effect of this highly questionable manoeuvre has been to heighten the level of indiscriminate repression to the extent that some villages have been entirely destroyed and hundreds of sympathisers — although absolutely not implicated in the tourist attacks — have been jailed in detention camps where torture has been repeatedly proven to be used. Long concentrated on the 'radical' Gemaa Islamiyya, repression was extended to the legalistic trend of the Muslim Brotherhood late in 1992.

As elsewhere in the region, the regime in Cairo keeps refusing any demand for political participation by any component of the Islamist trend. It has long succeeded in doing this, especially vis-a-vis the West, by emphasising the need to 'fight against the religious strife' between Copts and Muslims and 'preserve unity of the Egyptian society'. Western media also tends - sometimes too automatically - to connect any kind of anti-regime violence to its supposed 'religious strife' dimension. In fact, a close look at both the chronology and the causalities of these confrontations reveals that the 'religious' factor appears far from being the main source of violence, nor does it appear to be its principal means of expression. The involvement of Sudan or Iran, used throughout the summer of 1992 by the regime as a pretext, has no higher level of credibility. But it allows the regime to persist in denying access to the institutional system to all of its Islamist opponents, i.e. to the overwhelming majority of its opposition.

Almost throughout the Arab world, a regime's initial repression is countered by violence from the Islamist movements, creating a dynamic that characterises the present predicament, and largely determines prospects for the near future.

If the attitude of the Algerian regime is difficult to predict since it partly depends on the reactions of the international community, and especially on those of the West, it is a less ambitious project to trace the probable limits of its effectiveness. The Algerian leaders may be able to ward off the expression of the political majority that was manifestly demonstrated in the election on December 26th 1991, but how long they can do this will probably be measured in months, rather than years. And they will not be able to alter the balance of forces significantly. It is therefore hard to see how the march of the leaders of the FIS towards power can be interrupted for very long. Having destroyed the backbone of the movement, Tunisia can probably create some kind of apparently static situation for a while, although the attitude of the army can here like anywhere else influence the situation at any time. Like Tunisia, Egypt will have to maintain a growing level of repression here and there and the price of this violence will inevitably be paid by the system some day.

Since Nasser and the crushing of the Muslim Brotherhood, a great deal of water has flowed beneath the bridges of the Nile, and it is now generally admitted everywhere in the region that attempts to use force to remove a movement from the political landscape, especially when it is supported by a vast majority of the population, are most likely to be unsuccessful. Nevertheless, neither those in the North nor (although more understandably) those in the Arab political classes, seem in a hurry to accept what seems to be an inevitable cohabitation.

The image of the entire Islamic phenomenon still seems to be based on a mere extrapolation of the political style of the assassins of Sadat. One pretends to ignore the fact that its social setting has long outgrown the small groups of literalist and totalitarian followers of a religious discourse' in the strictest sense.

The Algerian voting booths, however, revealed more in a few weeks about the Islamist currents than most of the thousands of pages that have been written concerning them. The Algerian election of December 1991 was not only conclusive in exploding the theses of the existence of 'small groups afraid of marginalisation by free elections' and consequently tempted to seize power by force. It also demonstrated that the vast majority of women decided to vote for the FIS and with no less deliberation than their counterparts who voted for the secular parties. This expels another common fallacy, the simplistic prediction of an Islamist mobilisation 'against women'. Failing to find a 'third force' in the political landscape capable of combating the supposed enemy, external observers have been no less determined to pursue their desperate hunt for a segment of society (women, sufis, Berbers, militaries?) that can stave off the predictable results of the elections. The most obstinate analysts keep trying to sound out the battalions of abstentionists. Do they constitute an alternative majority? Most certainly not. How is it possible to forget that the elections which carried the FIS to its communal victory, and then to its semi victory in the legislative elections were the first in the history of independent Algeria (and for that matter in the entire history of Algeria, with the exception of the referendum on independence) in which the government did not simply falsify the level of participation, either through its party operatives, or through administrative ruses? Moreover, nothing suggests that the abstentionists would have acted as anything other than a simple echo chamber for the majority who voted, in other words would have served as anything other than a supplementary reserve of Islamist votes.

Toward Democracy?

When it comes to appreciating the capacity of the political forces in the Arab world to follow the long process of constructing tolerant societies, all that can be stressed clearly is that the line that isolates the 'good' from the 'bad', the tolerant from the intolerant, the democrats from the anti-democrats, those who defend human (or women's) rights and those who only accord a moderate interest in those directions, is infinitely more sinuous than the dividing line that distinguishes the Islamist currents from the rest of the political scene. Simply being Islamist is most certainly not a guarantee that one will be up to keeping promises of tolerance made by most Islamist leaders.

But in the same way, the simple fact of being anti-Islamist (like Saddam Hussein) or a Berber, or whatever, is no guarantee that one has a right to claim membership in this 'democratic camp' of which the West has all too often automatically accorded the monopoly of representation either to the elites in power or to those 'secularist' formations which the Islamist resurgence has irresistibly marginalised.

In conclusion, we will restate the hypothesis we have proposed: nearly everywhere in the Arab world today, it is the forces emanating from the vast movement of political Islam which appear to be the leading candidates to replace the regimes linked to the nationalist movements. But this assessment of the centrality of the Islamist forces only makes sense if one avoids giving the label 'Islamist' the limited and narrow definition — which we have already tried to show is not operational — of a movement linked to a precise ideology, to a specific programme, to modes of action determined and intangible, and eventually to a definite social base. Neither does the declaration of the preponderance of Islamist forces imply the 'superiority' of one political theory over another. What it wants to assess is the simple fact that in the Muslim world, the demand made to the West by a non-western culture of 'acceding to universality' from inside its own symbolic system, which expresses itself in this profound process of reconnecting with the 'pre-colonial' symbolic universe, is bound to affect the entire political chess board. Therefore shall we suggest that the analyses of the two major processes underway in this region, ie. of reconnecting the political discourse with the 'pre-colonial' symbolic system on one side, and developing political attitudes respectful of a pluralist culture on the other, ought to be clearly disconnected, so that at least we do not automatically consider the first as a mere obstacle to the second.

To pinpoint the nature of the forces which will assume the leadership of this vast movement more precisely would in fact require a heavy dose of 'clairvoyance', something that is forbidden to researchers. The most which can be done is to indicate the direction in which research must concentrate. Rather than focusing on the forces that are irresistibly marginalising themselves by being too far removed from the process of re-Islamisation, it is most probably much more efficient to investigate the internal dynamics of this Islamist resurgence, ie. the internal dynamic of each of its numerous components as well as the changes in the balance of forces between them.

It is in these dynamics more than anywhere else that one can begin to see the contours of the new forces that will assume the responsibility for directing these societies towards the twenty first century. Nothing today allows the analyst to assume that they will prove — politically or economically — any less efficient than their predecessors.

Notes:

* Burgat, Francois and Dowell, William -- "The Islamic Movement in North Africa' ; University of Texas Press.

POWER-SHARING ISLAM

THE INSIDERS' PERSPECTIVES

This chapter consists of three papers contributed by Islamic political thinkers.

In the first paper entitled "Participation in a non-Islamic Government", Sheikh Rachid Al-Ghannouchi discusses the principle of power-sharing. He refers to evidences from the Holy Qur'an and the Traditions of Prophet Muhammad and quotes Islamic scholars of jurisprudence to prove that although the Islamic State is the long-term target of the Muslims, participation in a non-Islamic government may - under certain circumstances - be the only viable option. He concludes that the current crisis in the Muslim world does not lie in convincing the Muslims of power-sharing but in convincing existing regimes of recognising the Other.

In the second paper entitled "Political Pluralism from an Islamic Perspective", Dr. M. Salim Al-Awa discusses the concept of pluralism from an Islamic point of view and concludes that political pluralism in a Muslim society is a necessity.

In the third paper entitled "Islam and Democracy – Mutually Reinforcing or Incompatible?', Dr. Hassan Al-Alkim discusses the concepts of democracy and *shura* and compares modern democratic institutions and procedures with the Islamic political institutions and procedures that are based on the concept of *shura*. He concludes that Islam and democracy are compatible.

THE PARTICIPATION OF ISLAMISTS IN A NON-ISLAMIC GOVERNMENT*

Rachid Ghannouchi

Introduction:

This paper attempts to answer the question related to the position of Islam regarding the participation of its followers in establishing or administering a non-Islamic regime.

Prior to attempting to provide an answer to this question certain facts need to be underlined:

First: the fact that a concept for an Islamic government does exist, and that it is the religious duty of Muslims, both individuals and groups, to work for the establishment of such a government.

Second: the fact that such an Islamic government, in the circumstances under discussion, is non-existent, and that had it been in existence, a Muslim would have no option but to support it and work for the reformation of such elements of corruption as might exist within it.

Third: the fact that the present circumstances do not seem to favour the establishment of an Islamic government. So much effort has been exerted in order to establish such a government, and despite their failure so far, it is the duty of all Muslims to continue the effort and cooperate in order to fulfil Allah's commandment and establish justice on earth.

The Holy Qur'an says:

"O you who believe! stand out firmly for Allah, as witnesses to fair dealing, and let not the hatred of others towards you make you swerve to wrong and depart from justice. Be just, that is next to piety, and fear Allah. For Allah is well-acquainted with all that you do." (5:8)

In the same chapter, verse 49 reads: "Judge between them by what Allah has revealed, and follow not their vain desires", while verse 44 reads: "Those who do not judge by what Allah has revealed, they are unbelievers."

Exceptional circumstances:

The scope of this discussion does not apply to the normal situation when the Muslim community can establish the system of its intellectual, political, economic, international and other relations on the basis of Islam and in conformity with its faith and cultural heritage — the heritage which continues to be deep-rooted in the hearts and souls of Muslims despite the attempts of Western colonial occupation to undermine its fundamental principles.

The discussion here focuses on the exceptional situation when the community of believers is unable to accomplish its goal of establishing the Islamic government directly. In this case the community is faced with tough options.

Realism and flexibility are among the most important features of Islamic methodology. These features explain the fact that this religion is an eternal way of life that is suitable for all times and all places. Furthermore, the lives of human communities, including the community of Muslims, are in continuous dynamism just like the life of an individual human being. Fluctuations between health and sickness, victory and defeat, success and failure, progress and slipping back, strength and weakness are only natural. Therefore, it is imperative that a religion which came for the purpose of improving the life of all humans wherever and whenever they exist should have the capacity to respond to all emerging situations and forms of development through which the Muslim communities may pass. And in doing so, such a religion would have to draw the main straight lines as well as the bending ones; that is it would not just be content with drawing the lines for the absolute fundamentals during normal circumstances, but would also define the rules and mechanisms which ought to be followed and observed during exceptional extra-ordinary circumstances. In this way the believers remain in close contact with the fundamentals of the Shari'ah (the revealed or canonical law of Islam) in the situations of both strength and weakness.

The Fiqh (jurisprudence) of requirements and necessities:

The Muslims' heritage of jurisprudence is the greatest and richest legal or canonical heritage ever possessed by any single community, so much so that the Muslims can justifiably be called the community of jurisprudence. The greatness of this jurisprudence stems from the fact that it is founded upon major legislative foundations known as *'ilm al-usul* (the science of fundamentals), which is a great Islamic science.

This science was studied thoroughly and developed over the years by highly talented and authoritative scholars. The apex of this development was reached by Al-Andalusi Ash-Shatibi whose studies and thoughts were complementary to those of his predecessor Imam Ash-Shafi'i. The learned scholars who dedicated their lives to this important realm of knowledge believed in the greatness of Islam; they thoroughly studied the revelation (Qur'an), the Sunnah (traditions of the Prophet) and the heritage of jurisprudence. They also took into consideration the various practical experiences and applications of jurisprudence throughout the centuries together with the sum of knowledge acquired by man during their own time.

Through this collection of the sources of knowledge, and in the light of their understanding of the purposes and objectives of Islam, they formulated a set of fundamentals for legislation whose ultimate goal is to serve the interests of man — the very essence of the message of Islam.

Ash-Shatibi says: "From our exploration of the Shari'ah, we have concluded that it was only set up to serve the interests of man. This is a conclusion which no one can dispute, including Ar-Razi himself. Canon laws were made for only one purpose and that is to serve the interests of humans in this life and in the hereafter. Allah says in the Qur'an:

"We sent you not but as a mercy for all creatures" (21:107);

"Allah does not wish to place you in difficulty, but to purify you, and to complete His favour to you" (5:6);

"In the Law of Equality there is (saving of) life to you" . (2:179) {1}

In his book Al-Muwafaqat, Ash-Shatibi details the types of requirements which Messengers were sent to fulfil in the lives of humans. He categorised them into 'essential requirements' without which life would be ruined; these requirements include the protection of faith, of life, of progeny, of wealth and of the mind. Then he spoke of the 'special requirements' without which man would be in distress and hardship. They include the requirement to enjoy lawful and good things in life. Finally, he spoke of 'ameliorative requirements' whose absence would not seriously undermine life. These include the various manners related for instance to eating and drinking etc. The fulfilment of such requirements is aimed at improving the quality of life. {2}

The general inclination in contemporary Islamic political thought is to adopt Ash-Shatibi's concept of the purposes of religion, namely that religion was revealed only to fulfil and protect the needs and interests of mankind in this life and in the hereafter, as a general framework for tackling new problems in the Muslim society. Within the framework of this general perspective or purpose of the Shari'ah, the details of religion find their appropriate place as branches of the fundamentals. Within the same perspective, all new problems in the lives not only of Muslims but of all humanity, can find proper solutions that guarantee the fulfilment of their requirements.

In this way evils can be averted without any need for violating the provisions of Allah's divine law, since this law already includes general principles from which new deductions can be made whenever life progresses or changes. Some of these principles apply to standard situations and normal circumstances, while others deal with exceptional situations and extraordinary circumstances. An example to the latter is the principle of 'necessities eliminate prohibitions' (necessity knows no law). This principle is a Qur'anic principle. Allah says:

"But if one is forced by necessity, without wilful disobedience nor transgressing due limits, then is he guiltless." (2:173)

Similar to this are the principles of balancing between the better and the worse and opting for that which seems to best serve the general interest of the people, and the principle of outcomes or consequences according to which acts are judged on the basis of what they lead to. The decisive criterion in all cases is the fulfilment of the needs of humans and serving their best interests. {3}

Power-sharing in a non-Islamic government:

The general rule in judging the acts of humans is that all actions are permissible unless a prohibition is specified. The prohibition in this case is derived from the commandment to implement the law of Allah and not to resort to adopting laws other than His. It is therefore a must for all Muslims to do what they can in order to obey Allah's commandment and establish His governance. But what if the Muslims are unable to do so? The rule is that we are obliged to do only that which we can:

"No soul shall have a burden laid on it greater than it can bear." (2:233)

The Islamic government is one in which:

1. Supreme legislative authority is for the Shari'ah, that is the revealed law of Islam, which transcends all laws. Within this context, it is the responsibility of scholars to deduce detailed laws and regulations to be used as guidelines by judges. The head of the Islamic state is the leader of the executive body entrusted with the responsibility of implementing such laws and regulations.

2. Political power belongs to the community (*ummah*),which should adopt a form of *shura*, which is a system of mandatory consultation.

If this kind of government is possible, it is then the duty of the believers to spare no effort in establishing it. However, if this is not possible, what must the community do?

On the basis of the general fundamentals of Islam and its purposes of accomplishing the needs and serving the interest of the public (and these include the protection of faith, souls, wealth and the prevention of evils), it is incumbent upon the community of the faithful to avoid passivism and isolationism. Every Muslim has a responsibility toward the task of establishing the Islamic government. If such a task is not possible, then Muslims must endeavour to accomplish whatever can be accomplished.

Power-sharing in a Muslim or a non-Muslim environment becomes a necessity in order to lay the foundations of the social order. This power-sharing may not necessarily be based on Islamic Shari'ah law. However, it must be based on an important foundation of the Islamic government, namely Shura, or the authority of the *ummah* (community), so as to prevent the evils of dictatorship, foreign domination, or local anarchy. Such a process of power-sharing may also aim to achieve a national or a humanistic interest such as independence, development, social solidarity, civil liberties, human rights, political pluralism, independence of the judiciary, freedom of the press, or liberty for mosques and Islamic activities.

Can any Muslim community afford to hesitate in participating in the establishment of a secular democratic system if it is unable to establish an Islamic democratic one? The answer is no. It is the religious duty of the Muslims, as individuals and as communities, to contribute to the efforts to establish such a system. In this way, the Muslims would seek the establishment of the government of rationale due to their inability to establish the government of Shara' - as Ibn Khaldoun put it. {4}

Documented Cases:

Several events can be quoted from the Qur'an, the Sunnah and Islamic history to prove that Muslims, as individuals or as communities, are permitted to participate in establishing or administering non-Islamic governments in order to achieve good and avoid evil.

In one chapter of the Qur'an we are told the story of Yusuf (Joseph) who was thrown into the well by his brothers and was then rescued, to end up in the Pharaoh's palace in Egypt where he was subjected to trial and seduction. It is worth noting that this young man, who was imprisoned and mistreated, seized the moment when it was right and expressed readiness to take charge of the most important office in the Pharaoh's government, believing it was his duty to rescue many nations that were threatened by famine and drought. He did not wait for the Egyptian people to renounce paganism and embrace his unitarian religion so as to form the foundation for an Islamic government.

What that young man had in mind was the fact that religion has come to serve the people and fulfil their essential needs. Yusuf had the conviction that rescuing the people from starvation and consequently from annihilation, could not wait. He saw that he was able to help, and he did help. Through his effective participation in administering the affairs of the people he performed his other responsibility of calling for Islam and admonishing the people to reform their lives and renounce evils.

The detailed narration of the story of Yusuf in the Qur'an is a clear testimony that his approach is commendable. What happened with Yusuf can happen to Muslims anywhere and at any time. In similar circumstances, Muslims have no option but to participate politically in establishing and administering non-Islamic governments in order to serve the interests of the *ummah* (community) and prevent evils. Failing to do so will lead to undermining these interests and to allowing evils to spread and dominate society.

The second example is that of the Negus (the Emperor of Ethiopia) who lived during the early years of Islam. The Prophet advised some of his companions who were being severely persecuted to migrate to Abyssinia descriibng the Negus as "the King in whose country none is wronged." The presence of the small Muslim community in Abyssinia resulted in the Negus embracing Islam, although he did not effect any amendments to his government in the direction of implementing the Shari'ah, as such an attempt could have threatened his kingship and endangered the lives of his guests. The story of that noble king has been documented in Islamic history and continues to be narrated to this day. The Prophet instructed his followers to perform a prayer for the King's soul when the news of his death reached them.

Commenting on this, Ibn Taymiyah said, "We know definitely that he could not implement the law of the Qur'an in his community because his people would not have permitted him to. Despite that, the Negus and all those who are similar to him found their way to the pleasure of Allah in eternity although they could not abide by the laws of Islam, and could only rule using that which could be implemented in the given circumstances. {5}

The third example is that of *hilf al-fudul*, that is the pact or alliance of *al-fudul*. It was an agreement among several pre-Islamic Arab tribes to support the wronged, maintain close relations with relatives and take good care of them. The Prophet did witness the signing of the alliance prior to his prophethood, and said afterwards that if he were to be invited to a similar alliance in Islam he would have accepted without reservation. He further stressed that any good and noble contract made in *jahiliyah* (the pre-Islamic era) is automatically endorsed by Islam. {6} It is thus concluded that the community of believers may participate in an alliance aimed at preventing injustice and oppression, at serving the interests of mankind, at protecting human rights, at recognising the authority of the people and at rotating power-holding through a system of elections. The faithful can pursue all these noble objectives even with those who do not share the same faith or ideology.

The fourth example is that of Omar ibn Abdul-Aziz. This Ommiad Caliph, whose rulership did not exceed two years, is considered by historians and scholars to be the fifth guided Caliph because of his piety and justice, although more than half a century separated him from the last of the four guided Caliphs. Although he was a king who inherited kingship, he was unhappy with the monarchy, and in principle did not approve of it. However, he could not alter the system and was unable to restore the right of the *ummah* in a consultative style government due to the accumulation of corruption over the years. Nonetheless, he managed to significantly reform many bad practices, and restored justice and fairness. By accepting the monarchy, which he did not approve of, he was able to do many good things, and no one said he was wrong or misguided in his actions.

Contemporary Considerations:

An Islamic government is based on a number of values which if accomplished in their totality, would result in a perfect or near-perfect system. But it may not be possible for all such values to be implemented, and therefore some must suffice in certain circumstances in order for a just government to exist. A just government, even if not Islamic, is considered very close to the Islamic one, because justice is the most important feature of an Islamic government, and it has been said that justice is the law of Allah.

Ibn 'Aqil defined *As-Siyasah Ash-Shar'iyah* (Islamic administrative policy) as the actions which bring the people closer to good and distance them from evil, even if such actions were not advocated by the Prophet or revealed from the Heavens.

He further explained that describing these actions using the phrase "those that conform with the Islamic law (*shar'*)" in order to imply that such actions should not contradict the Shar', is justified. However, if one means by such a phrase that such actions must specifically be mentioned in the Qur'an or the Sunnah (traditions of the Prophet), then this is wrong and can be taken to imply that the companions of the Prophet themselves went wrong. After all they initiated many new policies and took numerous measures in order to fulfil the needs of the society in response to new developments or changing circumstances. {7}

In contemporary times, numerous examples can be cited to show that Islamic individuals and groups have entered into alliances in order to prevent evil or in order to serve the community within a non-Islamic framework. This is happening despite the fact that many scholars still insist that such measures should not be pursued.{8} With due respect, these scholars make life difficult for the Muslims unnecessarily. Their opinions impose restrictions on a policy which is definitely permissible and lawful, and which is intended to equip the Muslims with the ability to react positively in situations that can be very difficult indeed.

To cite only a few examples of such situations:

First: About one third of the Muslims in the world are minorities in the countries they live in, that is to say they have no hope in the foreseeable future of governing their countries in an Islamic way. Many of these Muslim minorities face threats of exile or annihilation due to ethnic cleansing and other pressures. What options does Islamic jurisprudence have for them? Some people have been suggesting that such minorities should emigrate to countries that have Muslim majorities. If this was possible, and it is normally impossible, what good will it do them? Or is such a suggestion another plot against the Muslims in order to drive them out of their homes? There are those who advise Muslim minorities to isolate themselves and wait, but this too contradicts the very essence of the Islamic message which encourages the faithful to be positive, active and involved.

The best option for such minorities is to enter into alliances with secular democratic groups. They can then work towards the establishment of a secular democratic government which will respect human rights, ensuring security and freedom of expression and belief — essential requirements of mankind that Islam has come to fulfil.

The accomplishment of such important values in any society will immediately transform it, in the Islamic conception, from *darul-harb*, a land of hostility and war against Islam, to a land of peace and tranquillity. Al-Imam An-Nawawi defines the land of hostility (*darul-harb*) as the country in which the faithful cannot practice their religious duties freely, and consequently emigrating from it becomes an imperative duty.{9} True democracies are not like this; they guarantee the freedom of worship and belief.

Second: There are many Islamic communities or movements that exist in countries that have Muslim majorities but which happen to be ruled by dictatorships claiming to be Islamic or by dictatorships hostile to Islam. Such Islamic movements may not be able to reform the regime or change it alone. Does the *shari'ah* (Islamic Law) object to cooperation and alliance between these movements and secular parties that also work and struggle to topple the dictatorships and establish secular democracies that would respect humans and guarantee their liberties? No, not at all.

Third: Similarly, the Islamic groups which exist in Muslim majority countries governed by dictatorships may be able to attract majority support from the public and establish an Islamic government. However, such a transition may incite hostility towards them from within their own country or from other countries, rendering the newly-formed Islamic government susceptible to oppression or other forms of pressures that may end with its collapse.

Is there any reason why such groups cannot agree or coordinate with secular groups in order to isolate the existing oppressive power and establish a secular democracy postponing the long-term objective of establishing an Islamic government until circumstances permit? Certainly, there is nothing against that.

It should be emphasised that the choice in this case is not between an Islamic government and a non-Islamic one, but between dictatorship and democracy.

Fourth: The Islamic groups which exist in countries colonised by foreign powers. Is there any reason why they should not form a united front with the secular groups in order to confront the common enemy in favour of a national alternative, in which the Muslims would have a better life than under the colonial authority? Certainly, there is nothing to prevent them from doing so.

Conclusion:

If the establishment of the Islamic government is the short or long-term goal of every Islamic group in order to implement Allah's commandments, the *shari'ah* (Islamic Law) does take into consideration the possibility that such a goal may not be easily accomplished, and therefore an alternative is provided. Under exceptional circumstances, Islamic groups may forge alliances with non-Islamic groups in order to establish a pluralistic government system in which power is held by the majority party.

Such an alliance may also exist for the purpose of deterring aggression or getting rid of a dictatorship. In all cases, the alliance must not include provisions that would in any way undermine Islam, or impose restrictions on those who work for Islam and who seek to establish its system in the land. {10}

These arguments are based on:

- the principle of supporting that which brings good and suppressing that which produces evil,
- the rule that what an imperative duty is essentially dependent on is imperative in itself,
- the rule of consequences or outcomes,
- the principle of necessity.

What is most important is that a Muslim must remain positive and actively engaged in the effort to implement the revealed laws of Allah, whether partially or in their totality, depending on circumstances and resources. The essence of Allah's laws, for which all divine messages were sent, is the establishment of justice for mankind.

"We sent aforetime our Messengers with clear signs and sent down with them the Book and the Balance (of right and wrong), that men may stand forth in justice." (57:25)

It should however be emphasised that the problem facing the concept of power-sharing does not lie in the difficulty of convincing the Islamists to accept democracy, pluralism and power-sharing. The current general trend in Islamic circles is to adopt power-sharing - even in a secular style government - as a means for achieving mutual goals such as national solidarity, respect for human rights, civil liberties, cultural, social and economic development, and the deterrence of external threats.

The real problem lies in convincing the 'other', that is the ruling regimes, of the principle of 'the people's sovereignty' and of the right of Islamists - just like other political groups - to form political parties, engage in political activities and compete for power or share in power through democratic means.

The punishment of the Islamic victors in the Tunisian and Algerian elections - which have regrettably been taking place with the consent of Western democracies and the support of local 'secular theological elites' {11} that are allied with the oppressive regimes in both countries - provides a decisive evidence that the root of the problem in the Muslim world lies in the hegemony of despotism. Our main task now is to combat despotism in favour of a genuine and true transition to democracy.

Notes:

* Translated from Arabic by Azzam Tamimi

{1},{2} and {3}: Abu Ishaq Ash-Shatibi, Al-Muwafaqat 2/6-8

{4}: Ibn Khaldoun, Al-Muqaddimah

{5}: Ibn Taymiyah, Al-Fatawa 19/218-219

{6}: Sahih Muslim & Abu Dawud

{7}: Abn Qayim Al-Jawziyah, At-Turuq Al-Hikmiyah p13

{8}: -Maudoodi, The Islamic Government
-Dr. M. Abu Faris, Tahrim Al-Musharakah Fil-Hukumah

{9}: Imam An-Nawawi, The Forty Traditions

{10}: Dr. Salah As-Sawi, Political Pluralism in Islam p.142

{11}: Dr. Bashir Nafi', Article in Al-Hayat No. 10984 of 9 March 93

POLITICAL PLURALISM FROM AN ISLAMIC PERSPECTIVE*

Muhammad Salim Al-Awa

In essence, pluralism means the recognition of diversity. Not only is it a reality which no sensible person can deny, but is a legitimate right for those with whom we may disagree or differ; a right that no person or authority can deny or take away. Pluralism usually takes an adjective derived from the topic of concern, and thus can be political, economic, religious, racial, or linguistic.

Pluralism already exists in nature among creatures and among their various species. In this sense, it is an expression of the marvellous divine achievement.

Allah says in the Holy Qur'an:

"It is He Who has produced you from a single soul: then there is a resting place and a repository. We detail Our signs for people who understand. It is He Who sends down rain from the skies, with it We produce vegetation of all kinds. From some We produce green crops, out of which We produce close-compounded grain. Out of the date-palm and its sheaths come clusters of dates hanging low and near. Then there are gardens of grapes, of olives and of pomegranates. each similar (in kind) yet different in variety. When they begin to bear fruit, feast your eyes upon the fruit and the ripeness thereof. Behold in these things there are signs for people who believe." (6: 98-99)

Allah also says:

"Have you not seen that Allah sends down rain from the sky? With it We then bring out produce of various colours. And in the mountains are tracts white and red, of various shades of colour, and black intense in hue. And amongst humans and beasts and cattle they are also of various colours. Among His servants those who have knowledge truly fear Allah: for Allah is Exalted in Might, Oft-Forgiving." (35: 27-28)

There is obvious and significant pluralism among humans - in their races, affiliations, responsibilities, performances, talents, faculties and powers.

"Among His signs is the creation of the heavens and the earth, and the variations in your languages and your colours: verily in that are signs for those who know." (30: 22)

"O mankind! We created you from a single (pair) of a male and a female, and made you into nations and tribes, that you may know each other. Verily the most honoured of you in the sight of Allah is he who is the most righteous of you. And Allah has full knowledge and is well acquainted with all things." (49: 13)

In this verse the Qur'anic expressions of 'honoured' and 'righteous' are used to indicate the existence of these who are honoured and those who are righteous, pointing to the fact that diversity is a reality, and that pluralism in the Divine scheme of evaluation does not necessarily mean accepting the members of a certain category while rejecting the members of other categories. By categories I mean the grades of 'righteousness' and 'honour', which are based on sincerity of belief and clarity of conviction.

If one recognises the pluralistic nature of humans, and recognises their rights to disagree and differ, one must inevitably, and without much effort, recognise pluralism in the political sphere. Why should this matter require clarification? And why does it seem to many observers of Islamic political thought that it rejects political pluralism and adopts monism, or the unitary vision, which in most cases leads to an unjust despotic rule or a permanent tyrannical government.

Islamic political thought appears to be distorted and misunderstood over this as well as over many other issues. There are usually three reasons for this distortion. The first is that writings on Islam and Islamic thought continue to be constrained by the unquestioning adoption of ancient writings (*taqlid*), copying them, building on them and considering them fundamentals and references for analogy (*qiyas*). These ancient writings describe the situation that existed during the times of those who wrote them, based on the writers' understanding and assessment. The judgement given therein is that of ancient writers based on their or their predecessors' interpretation or comprehension of the fundamentals of Islam.

The second reason is that writings on Islam and Islamic thought still revolve around the ancient occurrences in the history of Muslims. Researchers who tackle these occurrences in Muslim history usually pursue one of two ways. They either take an interest only in the best and most enlightened times, deriving lessons from them as if they were the entire history of the Muslims; or alternatively take an interest only in the worst events and gloomiest stages and then ascribe such gloominess to the entire history.

The third reason is that the advocates of an Islam-based reform for the deteriorating political, social and economic situations in the Muslim world do not bother to explain to the people the Islamic position with regard to the organisation of society. They avoid tackling essential problems and are usually content with the fact that they invite to the faith of the majority; the faith which they themselves believe in. They usually uphold true slogans but fall short of making the required effort to translate these slogans into reality. Many seek to justify this attitude by saying they suffer security restrictions and are denied the right to form political parties. Some of the groups which pursue moderate policies function without governmental approval and therefore cannot be protected from arbitrary measures. These occur without prior notice and without obvious reasons. On the other hand, members of extremist (radical) groups are on the run and can be shot dead wherever they are ambushed. If caught alive, they are usually indicted and sentenced without proper trial or defence.

The three aforementioned reasons require some consideration. If *taqlid* (the unquestioning adoption of ancient writings) is generally bad, it is worst when applied to political thinking. Ancient writings that are copied and imitated by contemporary writers are 'relative'. They should not be referred to in order to restrict or hinder the progress of the Islamic political movements. These movements to revive Islam have been in motion throughout history and should continue to be so.

Islamic history, or the history of the Muslims, with all its ups and downs, is certainly a good source of lessons and admonitions. However, it should not be used to create restrictive precedents, which should be followed to the finest detail if deemed to be good, or which would cause Islam itself to be rejected and its followers denounced if they were precedents of tyranny and oppression.

The excuses made by those who call for an Islam-based reform are in essence valid excuses but do not justify their abstention from explaining to the people what they call them to. Nor do such excuses legitimise the adoption of obscure and inexplicable concepts which oftenly reflect negatively on Islam itself. Hence, the stand of Islamic thought toward pluralism requires renewed clarification. It is necessary to prevent any of the aforementioned reasons from causing the people to think that those who call for an Islam-based reform stand against political pluralism or support tyranny or that they are preparing for a new era of despotism cloaked in religion and protected by it!

It is important that those who call for Islam-based political reform do not miss the fact that the most extreme forms of oppression and the worst types of tyranny in history, were those resulting from the interpretation of religion so as to satisfy the ambitions or desires of oppressors. Many tyrannical practices resulted from the distortion of religions, introducing into them things that did not belong to them. The history of humanity, irrespective of religion, stands witness. Hence, it is important to underline the truth about Islam's position toward political pluralism. Islam considers 'differing' to be a genuine human right and an essential requirement of diversification.

The appropriate approach to Islamic political thought in contemporary times is - now as it has always been - to thoroughly examine Islamic fundamentals. The purpose would be to determine what the fundamentals obligate, and to suggest the means and methods believed to accomplish the fulfilment of such obligations. The means and methods that prove to be sound and reliable are endorsed, and those that prove to the contrary should be replaced. By doing so, we would be pursuing a sound jurisprudential rule, namely: "any course of action which fails to accomplish its targeted goal is invalid". {1}

The examination of Islamic fundamentals in this manner is termed *ijtihad*, which is governed in *fiqh* (jurisprudence) by scholastic aptitude, and in politics by the ability to serve the interests of the people. After all, securing the rights and liberties of the public is the essential foundation of obtaining good and averting evil.

Exercising political *ijtihad* for the purpose of organising and administering the state has never stopped throughout the history of Islam. However, whenever Islamic *shari'ah* was excluded from government, creative efforts to develop Islamic jurisprudence were frozen and jurists ceased to practise juristical explanation. Consequently, governors - as Ibn Qayim Al-Jawziyah put it - invented and introduced bad practices, thinking that *shari'ah* was inadequate or incapable of serving the interests of the people. Hence, Ibn Qayim Al-Jawziyah suggested that "wherever there is justice, that is the law and religion of Allah".

Others such as Ibn 'Aqil Al-Hanbali suggested that the Islamic policy is that which does not contradict the verdict of the Revelation. He stressed that those who claim that Islamic policy approves only that which is stated in the Revelation commit two mistakes: the first is that their claim is not supported in anyway by evidence from the Qur'an or the Sunnah (traditions of the Prophet), and the second is that by claiming this they put the Prophet's companions and their successors in the wrong. The companions and their successors did exercise whatever they deemed to serve the interests of the people so long as it did not contradict the Revelation. But they did not restrict themselves to the revealed texts alone. {2}

The question which we need to ask ourselves is: what do revealed texts or Islamic fundamentals obligate the people to do in the running of their daily affairs, and what do they forbid them from doing? Has a specific method been outlined in order for the people to fulfil such obligations and avoid such prohibitions? Before answering this question, one must testify that what *shari'ah* obligates must be observed. All such obligations must strictly be obeyed and failing to do so constitutes a major sin that persists so long as the obligations continue to be neglected or ignored.

To answer the above question, it is necessary to begin with emphasising that Islamic references do not outline a specific path for mankind to pursue in order to attain the political objectives stated in the Qur'an and the Sunnah.

The fundamental principles of the Islamic state can be summarised in the following points:

1. In neither the Qur'an nor the Sunnah does Islam prescribe a specific system of government. Nevertheless, it clearly defines the values and guidelines the *ummah* (community) should adhere to and rulers should abide by. In addition to other nomenclature, these values may be referred to as 'general rules' or 'comprehensive issues' {3}. In the political field, this is compatible with the nature of Islamic legislations which are characterised by complete flexibility. This in itself is an important prerequisite of applicability through extrapolation and deduction.

2. Choosing the ruler was the cornerstone in the organisation of the Islamic state when it was first established. Nevertheless, Islam at that time had only prescribed *shura* (consultation) as a method for making the choice. What matters is that the *ummah* (community) should be able to exercise its free will in choosing and appointing the ruler. This is exactly how the four guided Caliphs were chosen. The actual procedure is left for the community to determine, and may therefore differ from time to time and from one place to another.

Perhaps the best procedure in our time is the election of the head of state and of the people's representatives through direct free elections. All citizens should have the right to participate, and appointment to the office should be for a limited period. No group or individual should be excluded from the process or deprived of the right to nominate themselves or elect others.

3. Freedom is an indispensable Islamic value, guaranteed and considered to be instinctive. Political freedom, in Islam, is a branch of a general fundamental right: the freedom to choose. The Prophet said: "Let not any of you be a characterless person, saying: I do what the people do - if they do good I do good, and if they do bad I do bad."{4} Voicing one's opinion is not just permissible but is an Islamic duty. Scholars of *usul* (fundamentals) define a *wajib* (duty) as being "the action that is imperatively demanded" and consider a person who fails to execute such an action to be a sinner. {5}

4. Equality before the law and equity in the treatment of citizens and in the assessment of their rights and liberties are essential Islamic values. Such values should under no circumstances be abandoned.

5. Enjoining what is right and forbidding what is wrong are Islamic duties applicable to all fields of life. They are obligatory upon individuals and groups. Allah says in the Qur'an: "Let there arise out of you a band of people inviting to all that is good, enjoining what is right and forbidding what is wrong." (3: 104) He also says in the same chapter: "You are the best of peoples evolved for mankind. Enjoining what is right, forbidding what is wrong, and believing in Allah." (3:110)

6. Rulers are accountable to the community and are responsible for looking after its affairs. This responsibility was endorsed, in action, by the Prophet himself. No ruler succeeding the Prophet has the right to claim an immunity that the Prophet himself did not enjoy. {6}

In order for these political values to be accomplished in today's society, they require a guarantee of protection, and that is nothing else but political pluralism. This conclusion stems from the fact that Islamic fundamentals (sources) provide universal or general values which leave the *ummah* (community) unrestricted and capable of creative thinking and unlimited search for the best means of organisation and re-organisation. These include the means necessary for preserving the *ummah*'s right to live under the banner of Islamic values and for preventing rulers from becoming tyrants and oppressors.

It is only common sense that these means should vary from time to time and from one location to the other. For instance, a community that is under colonial control may have to resort to methods inapplicable to other places, or to means that were never employed by previous generations or other communities. Under certain circumstances, it may be feasible to borrow from the experiences and methods of other cultures if these are thought to guarantee and protect rights and freedoms.

In one of the best remarks ever made by a prominent scholar of Islam, Ibn Qayim Al-Jawziyah said: "Some scholars categorise government into *shari'ah* (law) and *siyasah* (politics) in the same manner as they categorise *deen* (religion) into *shari'ah* and *haqiqah* (reality), or as some may categorise *deen* (religion) into *'aql* (reasoning) and *naql* (tradition); but all these categorisations are wrong. Politics, reality, methodology and reasoning are all categorised into two classes: right and wrong. *Shari'ah* accepts and supports all that which is right and opposes and rejects that which is bad or corrupt. This is one of the most important and useful fundamentals." {7}

Islamic political thinkers are confronted with two arguments used by some Islamists when they talk about political pluralism or multi-party politics. Both arguments are easily refutable and do not in anyway undermine the credibility of the above discussion.

The first argument is the claim by some researchers that Islam does not know party politics. This, indeed, is a meaningless argument. If Islam does not 'mention' something, this indicates one of two things: either that it is not stated anywhere in the traditional sources or that Muslims have never practised it throughout their history.

In the first case, the non-mentioning of something implies that it is permitted. The only exception to this rule is the subject of worship which is not realisable or comprehensible by man, and in whose case non-mentioning implies prohibition. It is self-evident that political pluralism does not fall into the category of subjects that are beyond the comprehensibility of man; it is neither an act of worship nor a ritual of any kind. Actually, it falls into the category of changing circumstances in which interests are determined by logic and reasoning.

In the second case, the fact that earlier Muslims did not practise it is not a valid argument against pluralism. Even the very early generation of Muslims, the Prophet's companions, introduced new measures, means and methods that were not known during the time of the Prophet himself. It is only natural that Muslims should respond to changes and developments at all times and in all circumstances.

Furthermore, the history of Islam witnessed the birth of several political groups such as the *Khawarij,* the *Shi'ah,* and the *Mu'tazilah*, each of which then gave rise to various other sub-divisions. Such partisanship or factionalism became a common political feature of the Muslim society. Scores of different jurisprudential and ideological schools have emerged since the early days of the Islamic civilisation. They tolerated each other and coexisted. Therefore, there is no reason why political diversification or pluralism cannot be recognised and tolerated.

The second argument stems from the claim that the Qur'an has condemned factionalism, division and disagreement. Qur'anic verses are usually quoted to substantiate this claim. They include the following:

"They have cut off their affair (of unity) between them into sects: each party rejoices in that which it has." (23: 53)

"As for those who divide their religion and break up into sects, you have no part in them in the least." (6: 159)

Actually, this argument is nothing but a manipulation and a distortion of the Qur'anic text. As the Qur'an condemns 'parties' in these instances, it commends them in others. One can quote several examples including the following:

"As for those who turn to Allah, His Messenger, and the believers, it is the Party of Allah that must certainly triumph." (5: 56)

"...... they are the Party of Allah. Truly it is the Party of Allah that will achieve success." (58: 22)

"Then We roused them, in order to test which of the two parties was best at calculating the term of years they had tarried!" (18: 12)

It is clearly unacceptable to quote only the verses in which 'parties' are condemned, as this is bound to make one arrive at the wrong conclusion.

The other side of this argument is the claim some contemporary Islamists make, quoting Quranic verses which describe the *ummah* as a single community, to show that Islam does not permit the formation of political parties. They quote verses such as "Verily, this ummah of yours is a single ummah." (21: 92)

In fact what this verse, and all other verses that are similar to it, implies is the oneness in religion, which is sincere worship of and submission to the Creator alone without assigning partners with Him or below Him. Hence, applying this concept so as to imply political oneness, as opposed to political pluralism, clearly involves a distortion of the meaning. {8}

Contemporary *ijtihad* must inevitably arrive at supporting the concept of political pluralism, even if for the sake of argument, such a concept was not known before. Parties which call for that which is right and good, and which serve the interests of the public are included in the Qur'anic description of the believers "...... they are the Party of Allah. Truly it is the Party of Allah that will achieve success."(58:22) Parties which oppose the commands of Allah and His Messenger and which harm the interests of the public come under the Qur'anic description ".....they are the party of Satan. Truly, it is the party of Satan that will lose." (58: 19)

An Islamic state incurs no reproach today by licensing political parties and permitting political pluralism. However, it may - and probably it should - stipulate that these parties must abide by the values of Islam and respect its provisions. Apart from that, political parties are free to call for the political, social or economic programmes they deem feasible. Islam does not object to this state of affairs. {9}

Rather, I believe that the existence of political parties in the present circumstances will promote the progress and development of Muslim societies, and will bolster the freedom of expression in them. This will also serve as a safety valve to prevent despotism or check despotic tendencies. After all, most - if not all - of these societies have been suffering from some form of despotic rule.

The jurisprudence of Islamic fundamental principles is based on a grand rule, namely that "what a duty is essentially dependent upon is itself a duty". Is it possible for any political system to be set up at the present time while denying the people the right to differ or disagree, or denying them the right to the freedom of expression or the right to congregate and organise public meetings?

The only correct answer to this question is "no". The principles of Islamic jurisprudence, the logic of political interests and history stand witness to the fact that as far as Islam is concerned political pluralism is a necessity.

This conclusion should receive special attention by thinkers within the contemporary Islamic Movement and by those involved in political activities. On the one hand, it is our responsibility to explain the true position of Islam on these matters, but at the same time we should seek to gain the confidence of the public in order to promote the Islamic civilizational political project.

Notes:

* Translated from Arabic by Azzam Tamimi.

{1} Al-'Izz Ibn 'Abd As-Salam, Qawa'id Al-Ahkam 2/143

{2} Ibn Qayim Al-Jawziyah, At-Turuq Al-Hukmiyah p25

{3} Al-'Awwa, An-Nizam As-Siyasi, Dar Ash-Shuruq 1989
{4} Sunan At-Tirmizi, 8/170
{5} Al-Imam Al-Ghazali, Al-Mustasfa 2/18
{6} Al-'Awwa, An-Nizam As-Siyasi pp 231-237
{7} Ibn Qayim Al-Jawziyah, A'lam Al-Muwaq'in 4/375
{8} Refer to Tafsir Al-Jalalayn and Tafsir Ibn Juzay
{9} Al-'Awwa, An-Nizam As-Siyasi pp 76-77

ISLAM & DEMOCRACY MUTUALLY REINFORCING *OR* INCOMPATIBLE? (1)

Hassan Al-Alkim (2)

Introduction:

Debates on Islam and democracy have begun to acquirc a significant place in modern Islamic political thinking. (3) In their search for an ideological basis accepted by all parties in the Muslim world, thinkers from both the Islamic and secular sectors of Muslim society have embarked on a new mission to reconcile the differences between the various political groups.

The purpose of this paper is to examine the similarities and the differences between Islam and democracy. The paper is based on the hypothesis that Islam and democracy are mutually reinforcing. The paper is divided into two parts. The first deals with the theocratic elements in the Islamic state while the second deals with the democratic process. The discussion in the first part will include democracy, the Islamic state, the Islamic government, the concept of Caliphate, and the concept of Shura. The second part will discuss the election process, checks and balances, political parties, interest groups, political participation, and the rights of minorities.

Part One: The Theocratic Elements

Democracy and Islam

Democracy is a word derived from the latin word 'democracia', a compound of two syllables 'demo' and 'cracia', that literally means the peoples' reign'. The word has been incorporated in the English language as democracy, or the rule of the people by the people and for the people. Though such a definition sounds utopian, Robert Dahl argues, in his book 'Democracy and its Critics', that democracy is a polyarchy rule or the 'rule of the many'.

Western analysts have laid down a set of criteria as the basis for democracy, including the degree of political participation, elections, political parties, interest groups, separation of powers, checks and balances, respect for human rights, the rights of minorities, and the freedom of speech, press, practice and movement.

Among the basic criteria for determining the democratic nature of the existing political system is the free choice of the political elite which makes the three governing circles: the legislative, the executive, and the judicial authorities - this constitutes one of the main features of democracy. The process of selection is left open whether through direct secret ballot as in Britain or indirect selection through an electoral college as in the election of the American presidency.

Islam and democracy, though different in some respects, share a set of governing values in common. Islamic thinkers today look to democracy as a means or a mechanism through which the *shari'ah* (divine law) can be applied. However, they differ on two grounds: sovereignty and secularism. On the issue of sovereignty, Islam does not envisage sovereignty in the people or in the government. The Almighty God is the only sovereign and the people are only His viceregents. Islam also denies the idea of the separation of state from religion. This is due to the fact that 'state' in Islam is not an end in itself, but it is the stage preparatory to the hereafter, which is the final and lasting life. It is believed according to the Islamic traditions that people's prosperity will be achieved only through the application of the *shari'ah*.

The Islamic State

The Islamic state is a theocratic democratic state run by popular viceregency. It is based on a divine law and administered by the entire Muslim population. Its principles are derived from the Qur'an and Sunnah but its administration is supposed to be carried out by every Muslim. The entire population of the Islamic community is requested in one way or another to engage in managing the affairs of the state.

The form of the Islamic government, according to Al- Maududi, "is a divine democratic government because the Muslims have been given a limited popular sovereignty under the suzerainty of God. The executive power under this system of government is constituted by the general will of the Muslims who have also the right to depose it." (4)

It is a divinely ordained system of laws. The sources of the constitution of the Islamic state are divided into two categories. The first includes the Qur'an and the Sunnah. The "Qur'anic *shari'ah* was supreme to which obedience was due and rendered even by Mohammed". (5) The second source of *shari'ah*, Sunnah (the practice and sayings of the Prophet), was soon developed. However, the Sunnah occupied this position not only after the death of Mohammed but also during his lifetime. When Mu'ad ibn Jabal was sent to be governor of Yemen, he was asked about the basis upon which he was going to rule since he would be away from the Prophet's immediate guidance. His answer was that he would rule through the supremacy of Shari'ah and obedience to all its implications.

With the death of the Prophet and the end of the revelation and his practice, *ijtihad* came to constitute the third source of *shari'ah*. Thus the first two sources of *shari'ah* illustrate the theocratic dimension while the third reflects the democratic aspect in the legislative process. This is enhanced by the fact that no special group, clan, or even party play a paramount role in the functions of the Islamic state.

The Islamic Government

The Islamic government takes the form of a republic. It is initiated on the same basis as any other republic in terms of political institutions and political processes. The term 'Islamic', on the other hand, confers the ideological basis for the state. The fact that the Islamic state is an ideological state does not, however, negate the idea that it is a democratic state, since democracy is the most appropriate mechanism through which the *shari'ah* can be applied. Contemporary Muslim thinkers view democracy as a means to achieve an end. The difference between the Islamic government and liberal democracy lies in the fact that the former promises its people to comply with the *shari'ah* whereas the latter emphasizes its adherence to the worldly constitution and the fulfilment of the peoples wishes and aspirations. Abu Bakr aS-Siddiq, the first caliph, stated in his inauguration speech, "If I obey God and His Prophet, obey me, if I neglect the laws of God and the Sunnah of His Messenger, I have no more right for your obedience".(6) Therefore, "The Islamic government is a constitutional one but not in the same perception as the modern concept of the constitutional law. It is constitutional in the sense that the people who are in charge of it are restricted by sets of rules and regulations in the Qur'an and the Sunnah, which demand that people in the government obey, abide by and carry out such rules and regulations". (7)

The Concept of Caliphate

The Caliphate represents the corner-stone of the Islamic state. It means to cause the masses to act as required by religious insights into their interests. (8) The Qur'an says:

"Allah has promised to those among you who believe and work righteous deeds, that He will make them succeed (the present rulers) and grant them viceregency in the land, just as He made those before them succeed others." (9)

This verse clearly reveals that viceregency has been promised to the whole Muslim community. The idea of popular viceregency reflects a new idea of society - a society in which every Muslim is a caliph of

God. The concept of caliphate is based on the idea that every member of the society, regardless of colour, race, religion, or class, is an equal participant in this caliphate which does not tolerate any division based on distinction of birth or social status. In this form of a state, sovereignty is invested in the Almighty God whereas the authority to run the affairs of the state is delegated to the people. Ibn Taymiya emphasized the idea of popular viceregency by pointing out that the authority of an administration is vested in the people rather than the caliph since all members of the community are considered to be viceregents.

The Concept of *shura*

The concept of *shura* has been misinterpreted in western literature. The meaning of *shura* has been conceived as 'consultation'. *shura*, however, is a legislative process whereby the executive authority is obliged to accept the decisions of the legislative authority. It is a divine order since the Almighty God orders his Messenger not to make decisions except through *shura*. The Qur'an also describes the Muslims as those who take decisions through the process of *shura*. *Shura*, therefore, is an integral process in the function of the Islamic state since it is the only legal collective way through which the *ummah* or its representatives could enact or legislate laws or decisions related to the pursuance of its national interests. It constitutes the backbone of the Islamic political system. *shura* is defined as the process through which decisions concerning the state's public affairs are made. Such decisions are binding to the executive authority since *shura* is a divine order. (10)

Contemporary Islamic scholars call for the institutionalisation of *shura* through the adoption of representative councils or parliaments. Recruitment to such councils is open and measures adopted in the liberal democratic states are adaptable to the Islamic system. The only difference in the role played by the legislative authorities in both the Islamic political system and the liberal democratic system centres around the scope of legislation. In the Islamic political system the scope of legislation is limited to the guiding rule which should neither forbid good nor call for evil.

Part Two: The Democratic Process

Election

The *ummah* (nation) is the sole party invested with the right of choice. The free election of the *imam* (president) is a prerequisite for the bai'ah (contract) to be valid. (11) The Islamic state is based on the principle of no monopoly of power and the only way to ensure the fulfilment of such a goal is through elections. The Qur'an described the Muslims by saying: "And their rule is by counsel among themselves". (12) The Almighty God had instructed his prophet to "pardon them and ask protection for them, and take counsel with them in affairs of state". (13) In another verse Allah commanded His prophet " to make over trusts to those worthy of them". (14)

Islamic scholars like ibn Taymiya, ibn Khaldun, Abu Hamid al-Ghazali, al-Mawardi and others, agreed on the principle that the imam or caliph must be chosen by the people. Ibn Taymmia distinguished the caliph from the monarch on the basis of succession to power where the former is elected and the latter is self appointed by coercion. Al-Nassify wrote, in his book 'Al-Aqayd', that Muslims have no choice but to choose the imam who will execute the Islamic laws, defend the national frontiers, build strong armed forces, collect *zakat* and alms, solve domestic disputes and problems, secure justice, distribute the national income, take care of the elderly and the orphans and engage in *jihad* (holy wars).

Contemporary Muslim thinkers such as al-Maududi, Muhammad al-Ghazali, Sa'id Hawwa and the leaders of Islamic movements emphasize the importance of elections in the political process of the Islamic state. The president and those below him must be chosen by the people. (15) Hassan al-Banna, the founder of the Egyptian Muslim Brotherhood movement, called for a freely elected parliament in the 1940's. (16) Others argue for the necessity of a freely elected body with whom there must be regular consultation regarding the running of the government. (17)

Checks and Balances

Consideration of the issue of checks and balances helps in evaluating the democratic process in any given country. The Islamic government is a mixture of presidential and parliamentary systems. It has four organs: the presidency, the council of *ahl al hal wal 'aqd*, the council of *shura*, and the judiciary. The first three institutions are elected bodies and hence are directly accountable to the people. Members of the judicial authority, however, are appointed by the president, but the latter has no constitutional right to interfere in their business. The judiciary is immune from any influence unless its ruling is incompatible with the *shari'ah*. A further example of the judiciary's independence is illustrated in its power to call on the president to face charges.

Separation of powers constitutes another principle on which the Islamic government is based. The executive power is headed by the president. He is accountable to the upper house of the legislative authority, namely the council of *ahl al hal wal 'aqd*. This council plays the role of watch-dog and consists of an elected independent and neutral group with religious backgrounds. It interprets the constitutional articles and clauses, reviews the decisions taken by both the council of *shura* and the president, and solves any constitutional quarrel between the legislative and executive authorities.
"Although the *shari'ah* did not specify the form of the independent and neutral group to whom all the components of the society are subject, its decisions are binding whether they are in favour of the people or the president". (18)

The president's powers are restricted by the fact that he is obligated to consult with the council of *shura* and abide by its decision. (19) A bill introduced by the president must be ratified by the council of *shura* and endorsed by the council of *ahl al hal wal 'aqd*. Thus both houses of the legislative power act as checks on and balances with the executive authority. The president is also accountable to the people in general through the electoral process. Islam emphasizes that the people have the right to control their president and to advise him as well as to criticise him. (20) Therefore, the issue of checks and balances is fully in operation in the Islamic government.

Political Parties

Contemporary political systems may have a single party, two dominant parties, a multi-party system or no parties at all. It should be noted, however, that the idea of political parties is a recent political development and thus old Muslim scholars did not discuss the issue.

In contemporary Islamic political thinking, the idea of political parties has been disputed from one extreme to the other. Some Muslims argue that the idea of the multi-party system is not acceptable since the Islamic state is an ideological one and cannot tolerate the existence of parties with worldly ideologies. The counter argument is based on the idea that the Muslim society is a pluralist one that grants every member equal civil and political rights regardless of his or her racial, religious or social background. It is based on the value of equity. Thus, there are four arguments concerning the issue of political parties. Firstly a non-partisan system. This idea constituted the basis for the early thoughts of the Egyptian Muslim Brotherhood. Their rejection was based on the idea that political parties are man's thoughts and hence part of the worldly ideologies. Hassan al-Banna pointed out in what is known as *al-Islah* (the reform) that "true parliamentary reform will inevitably occur once all existing political parties are disbanded. The parliamentary system based on a non-partisan system coincides with the Islamic system". (21)

Secondly, the single party system argument is based on the idea that since there is an Islamic government, there is no need for other parties based on non-Islamic ways of thinking. Thus, there should be only one political party called the 'Allah's Party', which will carry out the social, economic, and political policies. "The party will not also face any internal dispute or feud that would lead to its split. There will be no struggle between the employer and his employee nor between the landlord and the farmers or peasants, nor between the governed and the governor, since all of them acknowledge the underlining principle". (22)

Thirdly, there is the Islamic multi-party system. The idea here centres around a multi-party system but all the parties must adhere to Islamic political thinking.

"God has given the right to the people to establish political parties to ensure that justice always prevails and to act as a guardian as well as a mean for political recruitment. But this must be under one condition, that the basis of the political parties is the *shari'ah.*" (23)

Fourthly, there is the multi-party system. The idea here is not to adopt the liberal democratic system that grants sovereignty to the people, but an Islamic system that will enable every group of people regardless of their political orientations to associate themselves with a political party, whose platform is not necessarily based on the *shari'ah.* Tolerance of peoples of other religious beliefs encourages more tolerance among Muslims with different political orientations. (24) This idea has come to be accepted by most contemporary Islamic political parties and movements. (25)

The fourth point of view is increasingly acquiring prominence in contemporary Muslim political thinking. The only condition laid down for the non-Islamic parties is to adhere to the state's constitution and this does not negate the idea of a multi-party democratic political system. Thus, contemporary Islamic political thought and democracy share in common the idea of multi-party system.

Interest Groups

Interest groups are the associational interests or pressure groups which specialise in the articulation of values and interests. Though the role of such groups has not been discussed in earlier Islamic political thought, examples of interest articulation can be traced to the days of the Prophet. The case of the woman who came to the Prophet and asked him to allocate part of his time for teaching the women is an example of such a role. A woman protested against the decision of Omar ibn al- Khattab, the second caliph, to place a limit on the dowry of women. Omar acknowledged the woman's point of view and retreated from his position. The above examples illustrate the role played by women, though they were politically unorganised, in the decision-making process, and could be used as examples of a pressure group.

Contemporary scholars see interest groups such as trade unions, women's leagues, teachers' syndicates and students' guilds acting as intermediaries on collective measures. Such groups should be permitted to form themselves into organised groups. (26) They argue that such groups play an important role in the decision-making process. Interest groups act as proper channels for feedback. Al-Maududi argues that there should be no law enacted concerning women without prior consultation with the women's league. (2) However, interest groups that seem to be self-seeking , that might lead to the monopoly of power, are not allowed to function under the Islamic political system.

Political Participation

The Islamic political system grants every citizen the right to engage in the running of state's affairs, to express his beliefs, thoughts, and opinions by all peaceful means under his disposal and to stand against oppression. (28) The Qur'an says: "Nor will ye worship that which I worship. To you be your way, and to me mine." (29) According to Khalid M. Khalid, "The people have the right to express their opinions and their propositions." (30) Contemporary Islamic political thinkers argue that the citizen of the Muslim state must enjoy "freedom of speech, freedom of criticism, freedom of practice and limited economic freedom." (31)

Based on the principles of popular viceregency and public involvement in the decision-making process in the Islamic state, the idea of referendum or plebiscite to promote mass participation in managing the state's affairs becomes an accepted method of decision-making, as long as such an act does not forbid the *halal* (permissible) nor promote the *haram* (forbidden).

Minorities' rights

Muslim scholars see the non-Muslims in the Islamic state as part of the community, linked by citizenship. Equality between Muslims and non-Muslims constitutes one of the main features of the Islamic state. Islam emphasises the unity among human beings by tracing them all to Adam.

Contemporary scholars emphasise equal civil and political rights for all the nationals of the Islamic state regardless of their religious beliefs. (32) The non-Muslims enjoy not only the right to worship but the freedom of movement to preach their faith. (33) The subjects of the Islamic state enjoy the right of private secrecy. The Qur'an says: "You who believe, enter not houses other than your own, until you have asked permission and saluted those in them." (34) Clearly this verse does not differentiate between Muslims and non-Muslims. The Prophet said, "he who hurts a non-Muslim, I am his opponent and whoever's opponent I am, I will litigate against him on the Last Day". Islamic history reveals the way non-Muslims used to be treated under Islamic rule. Omar ibn al-Khattab recommended his successor to treat the non-Muslims well. He said, "I trust whoever follows me with the good care of the non-Muslims, he must fulfil their commitments, defend them and not over-burden them". Omar was the first to incorporate the non-Muslims into the state's welfare programme. He instructed the secretary of *bait al-mal* (treasury) to review the *jiziah* policy (tax imposed on non-Muslims) and to abrogate the *jiziah* imposed on old people, children, orphans, and unsupported women and to give them social security benefits. Ali ibn Abi Talib, the fourth caliph, enacted a law equalising the non-Muslims with Muslims in terms of blood and money.

Conclusion

The preceding analysis shows that Islam and democracy are mutually reinforcing. Although theocratic elements are involved, Islamic political ideas do not involve complete rule by the religious hierarchy. The Islamic political system involves a great deal of political participation and shares with democracy many features of the democratic process. Thus, the Islamic political system is a theocratic democratic one - theocratic since it is based on *shari'ah* which constitutes the basis for the state's constitution and makes it morally binding . Democratic because the people enjoy the right of popular involvement in the managing of the state's affairs.

NOTES:

1 - A Paper presented to the conference on Power-Sharing Islam held in London on 20 Feb. 1993.
2 - Associate Professor of Political Science, UAE University.
3 - Fahmi Huwaidi, al-Islam wa al-Dimuqratiah (Islam & Democracy), **al Mustaqbal al-Arabi**, no. 166, December 1992.
Ali al-Kawari, Mafhwm al-Dimuqratiah al-mu'asrah (The perspective of Contemporary Democracy), **al-Mustaqbal al-Arabi,** no. 168, February 1993.
4 - A. al-Maududi, **The Political Theory of Islam,** 1939, p.22.
5 - For more details see Abdul Maqsud Abdul Fatah, **al-Saqifa wa al-Khilafa,** Kuwait, Nd.
6 - Cited in Khalid M. Khalid, **Khulfa' al-Raswul,** 1974, p.120.
7 - A. Khomaini, **al-Hukumah al-Islamiah,** 1969, p.41.
8 - Trans. by Franz Rosenthal, **al-Mogadimah,** London: Kegan Paul, 1958, pp.387-88.
9 - **Al-Qur'an,** (S. XXIV, v 55). p.914.
10 - Fahmi Huwaidi, op.cit, pp.16-21.
11 - Fahmi Huwaidi, op.cit, pp.12-13.
12 - **Al-Qur'an** (S. XLII, v38).
13 - Ibid (S.III,v159).
14 - Ibid (S.IV, v58).
15 - Muhammad al-Guzali, **Huquq al-Insan bin Ta'alim al-Islam wa Mithaq al-Ummum al-Mutahidah** (Human Rights between the Islamic Teachings and the UN Charter), Cairo: Dar al-Kitab al-Hadith, 1965, p.80.
16 - Cited in Dr. Richard Mitchell, **al-Akhwan al-Muslimun** (The Muslims Brotherhood), 1980, p.418.
17 - A. al-Maududi, **al-Hukumah al-Islamiah** (The Islamic Government), Cairo: al-Mukhtar al-Islami, 1976, 0.138.
18 - A. al-Maududi, **al-Hukumah al Islamiah,** op.cit., pp.137-38.
19 - S. Hawa, **Al-Islam** (The Islam), Beirut: Dar al Kutub al-'Almiah, 1979, p.292.
20 - A. Nafisy, op.cit, p.7.
21 - Cited in Dr. Richard Mitchell, op.cit., p.419.
22 - A. al-Maududi, **al-Hukumah al Islamiah,** op.cit., p.21.
23 - A. al-Nafisy, **'Andma Yahkum al-Islam** (When Islam Rules), London: Ta Ha Publishers Ltd., 1980, p.8.
24 - Fahmi Huwaidi, op.cit., p.13.
25 - **The Middle East,** No.103, May 1983, p.26.

26 - For more details see:
A. Najar, **al Iqtisad wa al-Islam** (Economics & Islam), 1983.
A. al-Maududi, **al-Hukumah al-Islamiah,** op.cit.
M. al-Guzali, op.cit.
27 - A. al-Maududi, **al-Hukumah al-Islamiah,** op.cit., p.273.
28 - Ali al-Kawari, **al-Mustaqbal al-Arabi**, no. ? February 1993, p.?
29 - **Al-Qur'an** (S.IX, v 5&6)
30 - Khalid M. Khalid, op.cit., p.250.
31 - S. Hawa, op.cit., p.290.
32 - Ahmad Abu al-Majd, **R'uiah Islamiah Mu'asrah** (A Contemporary Islamic Point of View), 1991, p.30, cited in al-Kawari, op.cit., p.32.
33 - Ibid.
34 - **Al-Qur'an,** (S. XXIV, v.27).

<u>POWER-SHARING ISLAM</u>

SUCCESSES

Few democratic processes have been allowed to succeed in the Muslim World and few regimes have agreed to hold fair elections. The main cause of apprehension has always been the strong rivalry of the Islamic Movements. In this chapter, the experiences of three Islamic Movements, which have taken part in successful democratic processes, are described.

The first experience is that of the Islamic Movement in Jordan. The first paper, which is contributed by Dr. Abdallah Al-Akailah, provides a brief historical background followed by a description of the power-sharing process and of the accomplishments of the Islamic Movement in Jordan.

The second experience is that of the Islamists in Kuwait. Dr. Nasser Sani describes the Kuwaiti democratic process and sheds light on the approach the Islamists are adopting in order to accomplish their objective of implementing *shari'ah*.

The third experience is that of the Islamic Party of Malaysia (PAS) which has been involved in politics for more than 40 years. In his paper, Mustafa Ali provides a historical background followed by an account of the PAS struggle to achieve its goals through parliamentary democracy, and of its achievements on local and federal levels.

SUCCESSES

THE EXPERIENCE OF THE JORDANIAN ISLAMIC MOVEMENT

Abdallah Al-Akailah

Introduction:

Following the collapse of the Islamic Caliphate and the abolishment of the Ottoman Empire in 1924, the Islamic and Arab worlds were subjected to fragmentation and division, resulting in the creation of several countries or states which were under the control of Western colonialism. This domination lasted until the beginning of the era of independence. With the end of the colonial era and the coming of independence the disappearance of the military presence of the West did not mean the end of Western influence. Indeed the political, economic and cultural dominance by the Western powers continued through national regimes of Arab and Islamic states.

The era of independence in the Arab and Islamic nations was characterised by the subordination and loyalty of most Arab regimes to the Western or Eastern blocs. Muslims perceived that their values, culture, civilisation and religion were in jeopardy because the political decision-making of almost all Arab and Islamic regimes was carried out in the capitals of the Western or Eastern blocs. The Muslims found themselves to be aliens in their own countries and homes.

The absence of freedom, justice, sense of responsibility, social equity and a system based on merit led to a deep sense of despair, which was increased by the prevalence of poverty, patronage, nepotism, unemployment, poor health care, crime and corruption.

Secularism was openly adopted by most regimes in the Arab and Muslim worlds. Society became polarised between a rich upper class of rulers or governors with their retinues on the one hand, and the grass roots dragging far behind on the other hand, without any middle class. The masses suffered economically but remained silent from fear of reprisals as well as in hope of an imminent change.

It was in these circumstances that the Islamic Movement was born, with the objective of meeting popular aspiration and the strong demand for reform and change. It soon became the agent for the restoration of Islamic life and the defence of the people's culture, values and religion, which had become threatened by the policies and practices of dictators and their totalitarian regimes.

The war launched by these regimes against the Islamic Movements varied in intensity. The onslaught included the banning of Islamic activities, lack of freedom of expression, and denying activists the right to employment and freedom of travel. Prominent leaders were executed and there was widespread torture in detention.

In Jordan, the situation is somehow an exception to the circumstances endured by the Islamic Movements in other Arab and Islamic countries. The Jordanian Islamic Movement was established in 1946, the year of Jordan's independence, with the aim of restoring the Islamic way of life in all areas of Jordanian society. The Movement focused on building up a new Muslim generation through education. Institutions specialising in social welfare and health care were set up and run by the Movement in various parts of the country to complement the work of its educational institutions and schools.

The occupation of Palestine by the Zionists has always constituted a great challenge for the Muslims and the Islamic Movement. This issue has always had an important impact on the political stand and message of the Movement. However, there are other issues which have received less attention. Examples of these are: the establishment of Islamic economic institutions, political involvement in the state's formal functions and the influence of the media in forming public opinion toward the Islamic programme of reform and change, which have unfortunately occupied a secondary position in the agenda of the Islamic Movement throughout the last four decades.

Active Participation:

The involvement of the Islamic Movement in politics during that period was confined to reacting to political events at local, regional and international levels. At the state level, the participation of the Movement throughout the past four decades was restricted to occupying a limited number of seats, that did not exceed five, in the Jordanian Parliament.

It was not until 1989 that the Islamic Movement emerged as a major political power at the local level when the Movement decided to take part in the parliamentary elections, which King Hussein of Jordan promised to hold pledging to guarantee fairness and non-intervention by official departments.

The Islamic Movement had run the election campaign efficiently and in a uniquely well-organised fashion by virtue of being a well-established organisation addressing the hopes of Muslims in Jordan. The Movement was the only group to announce the nomination of a list of 27 candidates and to ask the nation to vote for them all. A booklet containing the Movement's election programme and the names of all candidates was published and distributed throughout the country. The Movement won 22 out of the 80 seats of the Jordanian Parliament. Ten other candidates classified as independent Islamists were also successfully elected. As the Islamic Movement now constituted the largest single bloc of MP's, the new Prime Minister named by the King contacted them soon after the elections to ask for their participation in his government.

Negotiations started between the Movement's bloc and the Prime Minister. However, the Movement had to apologise and refuse to participate because its conditions were not accepted. The most important condition was the allocation of seven portfolios for the Movement including the Ministry of Education. In another political development, the Movement entered into negotiations with the Prime Minister over the vote of confidence in his government. The Movement set 14 conditions for granting a vote of confidence. These included the condition that the government should commit itself sincerely to the application of *shari'ah* (Islamic Law) in the spheres of education, economy and information media.

This was the first time that the Islamic Movement had taken such an initiative in the political arena. The people started acting and interacting with the newly emerging power. Islamists have become practising politicians whose participation in the so-called non-Islamic government was thought of as most unlikely before this experiment. Soon afterwards, the Islamic Movement took another political initiative by agreeing to participate in the Royal Committee for drawing up the National Charter, which was declared by King Hussein. The National Charter is a form of a social contract signed by all factions and parties in Jordan dealing with matters of interest to Jordanian society and covering their political, social, economic and cultural aspects.

One year later, the Islamic Movement found that the Government had not been implementing the conditions it had committed itself to. In fact, it was unrealistic to expect people with neither the willingness nor the qualifications to implement your conditions, meet your requirements, or take any serious initiative in that direction. Added to this was the fact that the Government itself was in a weak position, having failed to include any members of the major parliamentary bloc in the cabinet. Consequently, the Prime Minister re-opened communication channels with the Islamic Parliamentary Bloc, and asked for the second time for its participation in the government. This time his offer was accepted and the Islamic Movement was given five portfolios, namely those of Education, Social Development, Justice, Health and Islamic Affairs.

Six months later, the Gulf War ended and a new era of political developments leading to the so-called Middle East Peace Conference had started. The Islamic Movement made it clear to the Prime Minister that if any avenues for peace negotiations with Israel were opened, the ministers of the Islamic Movement would immediately resign. Eventually, the entire government resigned on the eve of the Madrid Peace Conference.

The next government that was formed then began looking for a vote of confidence. The Islamic Parliamentary Bloc in cooperation with other MP's in the Lower House made it clear that no government would gain confidence if negotiations with Israel were on its agenda. In the end the government did obtain a vote of confidence with a simple majority of 47 out of 80. Nevertheless, the new Prime Minister declared that he would not commit himself or his cabinet to peace negotiations with the Israelis. Two months following the formation of the new cabinet, the government announced the formation of its delegation to the peace talks. The Islamic Parliamentary Bloc met with other smaller groups in the Jordanian Parliament and formally signed a note addressed to the government. This stripped it of the confidence it had earlier gained because of reneging on the commitment. Forty eight MP's signed the letter, and when the ordinary session was resumed the government had no option but to resign. Then the present Government was formed. Since its mission was to supervise the Jordanian participation in the Peace process, the Islamic Movement's Bloc did not grant that Government a vote of confidence.

Through these developments, the Islamic Movement has gained experience and become more realistic. We have through this process been able to develop our calibre and practice. We have successfully been able to present a picture different from that deeply rooted in the minds of our opponents who continue to portray Islamists and Islamic Movements as fundamentalists, radicals and fanatics.

The achievements of the Islamic Movement's bloc during the first few years of parliamentary life are indeed numerous. To mention just a few of them:

1) the bloc participated positively in revising numerous legislations and making them consistent with the Islamic law,

2) the bloc cooperated with other political groups and with the government in serving the public interest,

3) the bloc won the position of the House Speaker after the first year of parliamentary experience,

4) the bloc participated in the formation of the Islamic Action Front Party,

5) the bloc played an important role in bringing about a lifting of martial law and the maintenance of civil rights and public liberties in the country,

6) the bloc has continuously voiced its support for the Palestinian cause and for other Islamic and human rights issues all over the world,

7) the bloc interacted well with local, Arab, Islamic and international developments,

8) the bloc stood firmly against all forms of corruption which affected both the public sector and government departments and institutions over the past four decades,

9) the bloc pioneered and led the opposition in the Parliament in questioning government policies and holding cabinet members accountable for every action seen as contradicting public interest.

Peaceful Coexistence:

A formula of peaceful coexistence has characterised the relationship between the Islamic Movement and the regime in Jordan since the early fifties. This has undoubtedly contributed positively to the power-sharing experiment in Jordan.

The factors of co-existence between the Movement and the regime are:

1- The Islamic Movement of Jordan understands the position of the Jordanian State and knows that its resources are very limited. The State's economy largely depends on foreign aid, and therefore there is a limit to what any Jordanian regime can do. Jordan is a very small entity created as part of the colonial process of fragmenting the Muslim world following the collapse of the Caliphate.

2- The Movement realises that Jordan lacks the essential requirements for the establishment of an Islamic state, and the regime is assured that the Islamic Movement does not seek to topple it or replace it with an Islamic regime.

3- The Movement, thanks to its social power and the services it renders to the public throughout Jordanian society, constitutes an element of security for the regime against any coup attempt. The Movement did play a positive role in the mid fifties in counteracting the leftist demonstrations which sought to topple the regime and replace it with a communist government.

4- The Movement regards the existing regime in Jordan to be a better alternative than all the leftist regimes which dominated other parts of the Arab World and repressed the Islamic Movements there.

5- The Movement constitutes a strong pressure group that expresses and defends the values, culture and civilisation of the Muslim community in Jordan. Its existence is thus respected and its activities are tolerated by the regime which is well aware of the Islamic nature of the people.

6- By virtue of its Hashemite descent, and contrary to what has been happening in other Arab countries, the ruling family in Jordan would never resort to brutal treatment or suppression of the Islamists.

7- The Islamic Movement in Jordan deplores violence and denounces terrorism. It does not believe in change by confrontation or revolution, but adopts a peaceful methodology based on gradual persuasion through dialogue. Such a policy is acceptable to the regime.

8- The regime and the Islamic Movement show a certain degree of flexibility in dealing with each other during crises whether the tension was initiated by the regime or by the Movement itself.

9- The Movement's methodology and approach are well balanced between its principles on the one hand and the limitations of the Jordanian situation on the other hand.

10- The demands of the Islamic Movement at most are reformatory in nature and encompass all aspects of life. However, they do not in any way threaten the regime or propose an alternative to it. Hence, the regime does not see that such demands constitute any real threat to its existence or stability.

The demands of the Movement can be briefed as follows:

- Freedom,
- Equality,
- Justice,
- Democracy and the necessity of respecting the choice of the people,
- Clean, responsible, sincere, fair and qualified government,
- The prevention of corruption and moral dissolution,
- The appointment of the appropriate person to the appropriate position,
- The combating of sectarianism and regionalism, and bolstering national unity,
- Support for and defence of human rights, and the rejection of repression and oppression,
- The denunciation of aggression and supporting liberation movements against colonialism,
- The adoption of measures leading to Arab and Islamic unity, and the establishment of various types of institutions that would build Arab and Islamic solidarity in the economic, political, military and cultural fields.

What do we want from the West?

We simply want a commitment to honesty, objectivity and a rational approach when studying or writing about the Islamic Movement and a commitment to quit the attitude of distorting facts and neglecting or ignoring realities.

We want the West to respect our right to freedom and our people's choice to adhere to our culture, values, civilisation and cause.

We want democracy and we work for democratic change. In our conviction the theme of democracy is compatible with our philosophy of Shura or consultation.

We are willing to cooperate in the endeavour to bring about a new human world order aimed at the achievement of a just, prosperous and well-balanced society in which human beings can feel secure and dignified and have their needs met. Such a world order is one which the Western civilisation has clearly fallen short of accomplishing.

We work according to the principle that says, "if you cannot have an ideal government, then make your own ideology more realistic." This can only be achieved through power-sharing and the adoption of democracy.

Will the West recognise this fact, and will it act accordingly ? We hope so.

102 POWER-SHARING ISLAM?

THE KUWAITI POWER-SHARING EXPERIENCE

Nasser Sani

I was invited to this symposium to speak about the Kuwaiti power-sharing experience. This must necessarily have reference to the word 'democracy', this word which is now regularly discussed and defended in many parts of the Third World. I was involved in a discussion the other day about a Middle Eastern country that is expected to be taken over by a new ruling regime. I was asked, "What would you say to the newcomers about what you believe to be an ideal model of government for the Middle East?" I responded by uttering the word 'democracy'.

Democracy, as everybody knows, is not something that you can adopt immediately, it is not a suit you go and buy and once you've put it on you become democratic. There are several stages for its adoption: as with a tree, you plant it and take care of it and afterwards you see the fruits of your labour. It takes time to cultivate democracy. I would like to explain how democracy has developed in Kuwait and how it has affected the society.

Democracy in Kuwait is well-stated in the State's constitution which talks about the existence of three separate powers. The constitution grants the legislative power to the national assembly (parliament), and distinguishes it from the other two executive and judicial powers.

1981 was the year when the parliament was re-assembled after being dissolved for four years. As the Amir maintains complete control over the three powers mentioned above in his capacity as the Head of State, he possesses the right to dissolve the National Assembly whenever he deems necessary, although of course he is requested by the constitution to abide by various conditions. The Assembly has to be reconvened within sixty days of its dissolution and the Amir has to call for a new election. What in fact happened is that the last time it was dissolved, the Assembly remained dissolved for four years in clear violation of the constitution. So when a new round of elections was held and the Assembly was reconvened in 1981 it was the first time that the Islamic groups had ever taken part in the elections, and the Islamic Movement won a couple of seats. It was the first time that candidates from the Islamic Movement had actively entered the political arena. The opponents of the Islamists at the time, that is the leftists, also participated in the elections but did not win a single seat.

The people started to call that 1981 parliament the 'Islamic Parliament'. It was not actually an Islamically-oriented parliament, so why was it nicknamed the 'Islamic parliament'? This was simply because thc newly elected Assembly members proposed an amendment to Article 2 of the Kuwaiti constitution so as to state that Islamic *shari'ah* would be the only source of legislation. The motion won the support of 48 out of a total of 50 MP's — undoubtedly a very good majority.

That Parliament managed to get new laws passed in favour of the Islamisation of Kuwaiti society. Among the most important of these laws was the law pertaining to what we call 'the *zakat* House'. This is a governmental body that collects the *zakat* (alms tax) and distributes it to people in need, both inside and outside Kuwait. Up to now this establishment has been one of the most successful institutions in that it does real work for Islam, rather than just talking about Islam.

In 1985 further elections produced a new parliament. Competition was very tough indeed, and representatives from different parties won seats. The majority of the seats in that parliament went to the opposition. There was intense conflict among the various parties represented in the National assembly and even in the Cabinet.

The 1985 parliament may be called the 'questioning parliament'. MP's started questioning a minister who was a member of the Royal Family. He was questioned in accordance with the State's constitution which clearly states that ten members of the parliament can call a minister for questioning. It further states that two weeks after the start of questioning, MP's should decide whether or not to grant the minister a vote of confidence. If a majority of non-cabinet member MP's in the parliament vote against the minister, he would be required to immediately resign his position. This is exactly what happened in that particular case, which was debated just one year after the beginning of that parliament.

The MP's went on questioning ministers one after the other. Applications for questioning were usually submitted by three different groups: the Islamic Movement, the left and independents. This grew into a genuine democratic practice involving very serious and tough political dialogue. In many cases, the questioning ended with the minister under questioning submitting his resignation. A couple of months later the Amir found the parliament interested in this game and wanting to question more ministers. Later on, there was a queue of up to four ministers awaiting questioning. Undoubtedly, this was perceived by some people as a misuse of constitutional powers. This eventually prompted the Amir to dissolve the parliament in 1986.

Parliamentary life was suspended for a period of six years during which no real democracy existed. Unfortunately, during the absence of parliament a lot of illegal measures were taken, and the perpetrators of these measures easily escaped punishment due to the lack of popular control and accountability. When the parliament was reconvened after the recent elections in October 1992, the newly elected members of that parliament started to open the files of the previous six years. It was clearly evident that during those six years power was one-sided, and even if the government intended to be fair it was not because of the absence of supervision from the people.

We found many things, historical, economic and political, that were against the interests of the country. Therefore immediately after the liberation of Kuwait, all political groups got together and signed a document in which they agreed on the future of the Kuwait they wish to see and live in. That was the first time in the history of Kuwait when all political groups unanimously agreed on a set of priorities. The first item in the document was their demand for the full implementation of the Islamic *shari'ah*.

There were indications of an inclination towards the *shari'ah* by most parliamentary candidates. This was a very healthy sign and almost every candidate who won a seat in this parliament did talk about Islamic *shari'ah* and included it in his programme.

There are now several recognisable blocs within the Parliament, for example the Constitutional Islamic Movement (CIM), the Popular Movement, the Nationalists and other smaller Islamic groups as well. However, as far as the overall strategies and policies are concerned, it is difficult within the Kuwaiti situation to differentiate clearly between the Islamic Movement and the other blocs, especially after agreement was achieved in the unanimously adopted aforementioned document, namely that everybody accepts and supports the full application of the Islamic *shari'ah*.

Therefore, we feel that the question of *shari'ah* implementation in this parliament is going to be given serious consideration. The *shari'ah* also needs careful cultivation, we cannot just say we want Shari'ah and expect it to happen. We have to provide alternative solutions to existing problems, and new economic programmes need to be devised. We cannot simply say we don't want interest and expect people to go back to their accounts and the international economy and fill the vacuum. You have to put forward the alternatives and actually put them into practice. You have to get Muslim scholars to solve all the technicalities that could face an Islamic bank to enable it to perform properly. To this end a special committee for *shari'ah* implementation was assigned a year ago. It is made up of an excellent group of scholars and they have good support financially and politically. They are trying to gradually prepare the ground for full *shari'ah* implementation in different fields. For instance, two weeks ago they had an international conference on how to Islamise the economy. In Kuwait we have one of the leading Islamic banks in the world called Kuwait Finance House which has 40% of the market share in the Kuwaiti banking market.

So what we could learn from this *shari'ah* argument together with democracy is that Islamic issues should be public. It is not an issue for just one group of people, it has to be promoted as a public issue for everybody. Dividing society into Muslims or Islamists against non-Islamists works against the lesson that we have learned by this experience. Islam has to be a public issue.

A second lesson we have learned is that we must promote professionalism. When we talk about Islam, we should let the professionals talk about Islam in their own fields, as I have just mentioned in the example about banking. I used to be in banking and I met a banker the other day visiting Kuwait who asked me how you could apply the concept of no interest in banking. I said we call it *murabaha* and explained to him that there is very little difference between it and the normal transection in traditional banking. He was very interested in that idea, but of course a real definition of *murabaha* has to come from a real life situation, from the counter in the bank, when a client comes in and asks how to use *murabaha* and wants to follow the *shari'ah*. So when we talk about professionalism we want those professionals who can produce real alternatives for the society, not just those who say, 'We promote *shari'ah*, *shari'ah* is the solution.' That may sound good in politics but at the end of the day you must have real examples set up by professionals to get the things delivered.

The third lesson we learned from this experience is the necessity of keeping in touch with the people. A lot of democrats and Islamists talk about these nice things in universities, giving lectures and so on, but as they are not close to the people, they do not know their needs. If you talk publicly about implementing Islam, your programmes have to solve the people's problems, otherwise someone who does not have health care will ask, "What is the meaning of this *shari'ah* you are referring to, I need to be treated." You cannot enclose yourself in an ivory tower, you have to stay close to and work with the people.

Nowadays in Kuwait there are many instances where democracy is applied and yet we still have to broaden the grounds for democracy. Women do not yet have the vote, and those who are under 21 are not eligible to vote. We hope the voting age can be lowered to 18, and a number of segments in the society are calling for the widening of the grounds for greater electoral contribution from the people.

In the economic sphere all future laws regarding the economy in Kuwait will be in accordance with the *shari'ah* and this is a very good achievement. It is a gentlemen's agreement between everybody in the parliament and I hope it will continue. Socially, a number of charity institutions have been established which are well developed locally and internationally. They are making very good contributions and keeping in line with the goal of working closely with the people.

So, how do I see the future? I think the future of this small country is closely linked to its neighbouring countries, and to the Middle Eastern region as a whole. I hope a real democratic movement will take place in a number of these countries so that in a couple of years we will not be speaking of democracy in country X or Y or Z, we will be able to come here and talk about democracy in the Third World. And I also hope that we will have a really good application of democracy, because I believe democracy well-applied always works for the good of the people.

THE ISLAMIC MOVEMENT & THE MALAYSIAN EXPERIENCE

Mustafa Ali

Introduction

It must be stated from the outset that power-sharing in itself is not the primary objective of the Islamic movements. It is just a strategy and a mechanism through which the ultimate objective ie. the establishment of an Islamic system of government may be achieved. It is in the light of this objective that the power-sharing experience of the Islamic Party of Malaysia (PAS) is presented, to add to the list of political experiences undergone by various other Islamic movements throughout the world. What is important is that the ensuing discussion and deliberation arising from this multitude of experiences should culminate in a well-defined plan of action which will give a new course and direction to the Islamic movements in their long and arduous struggle.

Religio-cultural and Political background

Islam came to Malaysia (then Malaya) in the late thirteenth century — relics in the eastern state of Terengganu bear evidence to this fact. Whatever the exact date was, what is more important is the form or nature of the conversion that took place, since this has had a direct influence in shaping the world-view and ethos of the people who embraced the religion. During that period the land was peopled by Malays with very small pockets of Arabs, Indians and Chinese in the port area of Malacca which had risen to fame as a key trading centre. Foreign traders who came to Malaya found Malacca an ideally located port for their trade in south-east Asia, especially when they had to rely on the changing monsoon winds to ply the east-west route between India, Europe, the Middle East and China.

The predominant culture was a Hindu-Buddhist mix with elements of animistic belief. Against this cultural background came Islam. The conversion began with the ruling feudal class - the kings known as Rajas - and the ensuing result was the replacement of the old Hindu-based feudal system with the Islamic-infused Malay Sultanate. Although it led to the immediate conversion of the subjects, in the political domain the total system of Islam was not evident. However, as a faith it became firmly entrenched.

Western Colonialism

In the early sixteenth century the first colonialist set foot on Malayan soil when the Portuguese captured Malacca after a brief encounter with the local Malays led by the Sultan of Malacca. The end of the Sultanate was not too surprising as Islamic principles had not been adhered to and under the absolute monarchy the Sultan could and did oppress the people. The people's subjugation to their ruler was more out of fear than awe. Chaotic conditions had prevailed when siblings fought for kingships and civil war had become rife. The Malays, thus weakened, were no match for the highly-motivated and zealous Portuguese who were bent on Christianising the archipelago. Later, when Portuguese influence began to decline on a global scale, the Dutch replaced them in Malaya. Later still in 1824 the Malay Peninsula was handed over to the British, based on a mutual agreement with the Dutch who exchanged Java for Malaya. The coming of the British had the most profound influence on Malaya because unlike their predecessors, the British wanted total control over the country. The Portuguese and the Dutch were only interested in the trade plying the Malacca Straits and were satisfied with a nominal presence in Malacca and its surrounds. The British however wanted to rule all of Malaya.

British Colonial Rule

British rule lasted for 133 years with an interruption of about five years during World War Two when Malaya came under Japanese occupation. The most significant development during the British period was the immigration of the Chinese and Indians from south China and India. The implementation of the British system of government then safeguarded these immigrants' interests, as well as those of the colonial British. Though this influx was more for economic purposes - that is for the development of rubber plantations and tin mines - the hidden motive was to create a multi-racial, multi-religious society that would be highly volatile unless well-controlled. In addition, the new society thus formed would hamper the Islamic movement if it ever attempted to change the western system of administration when and if the colonialists left.

Thus the new society was one of a majority Malay-Muslim base with an increasing immigrant population. Most if not all of the immigrants settled on the west coast and were instrumental in the development of the colonial economy. Malay Muslims were relegated to a very small role in the economy with the emphasis being on self-subsistent agriculture. Meanwhile, British policy and administration was the cause of Muslim unrest, leading to several uprisings and incidents led mainly by the ulama. The purpose of such opposition was to drive the colonialists off Malayan soil.

The Formation of PAS

The first Islamic movement to be formed was the Hizbul Muslimin. It was founded by Ustaz Abu Bakar al-Baqir in 1948. Since the policy of the movement was one of total opposition to *kufr* (infidelity) rule with the aim of establishing Islam, the colonialists lost no time in hunting down the activists and leaders of the movement. The Hizbul Muslimin was the precursor of PAS and despite its short history, it managed to awaken the Muslims to the true nature of Islamic struggle. However under heavy pressure, not only from the colonial administration but also the Malay Nationalist Movement — which colluded with the British — Hizbul Muslimin was destroyed. Ustaz Abu Bakar al-Baqir was arrested and all the other leaders and members had to go underground.

The vacuum left by Hizbul Muslimin was later filled with the formation of PAS in 1951. PAS was set up by an assembly of *ulema* (scholars) who gathered in the Northern Malayan town of Bukit Mertajam. The *ulema* felt that since UMNO — the dominant party of the Malays — had decided to base its struggle on secular nationalism, the Muslims had no choice but to establish a movement to struggle for the establishment of an Islamic state. Following its establishment, PAS played a crucial role in the independence movement. Despite constant harassment by the authorities PAS survived and its influence spread.

Parliamentary Democracy

The nature of the Islamic struggle in post-independence Malaya changed with the new political environment. A few factors that had and still have a bearing on the approach and the techniques employed by PAS must first be examined. Paramount in this scheme was the political set-up promising a Westminster style secular democracy in which political parties could participate in elections held once every five years.

The next was the Federal Constitution of Malaya (later Malaysia), that was promulgated based primarily on British interests — both short and long term — as well as on the traditional and historical background of the people. This means the elements incorporated into the constitution took into consideration traditional Malay society — the preservation of Malay customs, Malay rights, the Malay rulers and the Islamic religion. The Malayan political system thus evolved was one that maintained these elements but at the same time stressed the multi-racial charcter of the new nation.

The third factor could be seen in the implementation of the federalism concept in the Malayan administration. Under this system two distinct administrations were set up — one at the federal (central) level and the other at the state (provincial) level. Division of authority between the respective governments was clearly outlined with the states having their own constitution yet being subject to the federal constitution. One fact that needs to be noted here is that by creating a political environment and system that came to be accepted by elements of the local leadership, the British got off clean for their oppression during colonial rule and their removal of the pre-colonial system of administration which had been based on Islam in many of the states.

Political Strategy

The factors mentioned above had a direct effect on the political strategy that PAS would take from then on, to make as much gain as possible for the cause of Islam. In this contract the open political electoral system allowed PAS to operate as a party at political level while maintaining the basic strategies of any Islamic movement. The system also provided the possibility for using a 'peaceful' approach which was desirable until such conditions ceased to operate. A radical opposition would be proper only if circumstances changed, bringing for instance, the abolition of free elections and the establishment of an autocracy in its place. As a result of this PAS applied and continues to apply the 'peaceful' approach (*muwajaha silmiyah*). This approach is the guiding principle in its decisions to form liaisons with other groups, especially in terms of sharing influence or power.

The Incident of May 13th 1969

Immediately after independence multi-party elections were held. During the 1959 elections PAS made enormous gains by capturing the states of Kelantan and Terengganu despite having only managed to secure one parliamentary seat in the election of 1955. PAS continued to make good progress in the 1964 and 1969 elections, however 1969 was a watershed in Malaysian politics since the Chinese-based parties made tremendous gains and threatened the traditional balance of power in which Malay-Muslim dominance was assured. The 1969 results caused the non-Malay-Muslim elements to try to tip the political balance in their favour. The result was the tragic violence and disturbances of May 1969 that caused Parliament to be suspended until 1972. This incident was the major cause of the first power-sharing experience between PAS and another party — in this case the Alliance. The overriding consideration was the fact that Malay political power was under threat since the Alliance had lost badly to the opposition, particularly the Alliance's Chinese component, the MCA, which had been beaten by the fast rising DAP. UMNO in turn had lost to PAS in many areas. For UMNO, the political situation provided it with just the right formula to draw PAS into a coalition that would strengthen their political base, while containing PAS influence amongst the Malays. It should be noted that prior to the 1969 elections PAS was the sworn enemy of UMNO. It was to be discovered later that UMNO's thinking was that if PAS could be persuaded to join a new coalition it could be kept 'in check' whilst its Islamic credentials could be put into question with the passage of time. However, the most important and immediate concern was to save Malay political power and thus UMNO appealed to PAS to join the new coalition.

The First Coalition

As for PAS, in the short term the preservation of the political base in the hands of the Malay Muslims was the immediate priority. PAS accepted the offer to join the coalition despite opposition from many sections of its own membership during a muktamar (conference) in 1971 that hotly debated the matter. In a highly contested vote a resolution tabled at the muktamar was narrowly passed allowing PAS to join the ruling party as a coalition partner. In 1974, this loose coalition was transformed into a new coalition called the National Front in which PAS was also a partner. Despite still having Kelantan in its hands and a large number of seats in Terengganu and Kedah, PAS went ahead with the power-sharing experience. The coalition of 1971 was not a preplanned strategy but came about as a political necessity due to the circumstances described above. Neither PAS nor UMNO could brush aside the new political reality created by the incident of May 1969.

The coalition itself embraced every level of government administration right down to the local government. What needs to be examined is what gains PAS made and what in turn were the negative effects to the party and movement.

If pre-1969 PAS was the only party struggling for Islam, now with PAS participation in the National Front government, an Islamic veneer was given to the ruling coalition. PAS had hoped that under the accord reached between it and UMNO prior to the formation of the coalition, firm steps would be taken to bring about structural changes to the government that would then ease the path towards the implementation of Islam. Eventually it turned out that it was only an UMNO ploy to convince PAS to join the coalition and thus to contain its influence. Even the much touted Malay Muslim factor as the reason for inviting PAS into the coalition was only illusory. As mentioned above the prevailing situation provided UMNO with an excellent opportunity to cut down on PAS' influence.

As a result of the PAS decision to join the ruling coalition, in time any credible opposition from the Malay masses towards the inadequacies of the ruling party dwindled and ceased. Though PAS was in government, yet it was UMNO that was the dominant party making decisions on policy. The waning of opposition could be observed in the next elections in 1974 where many Malay-dominated seats were won uncontested by the ruling coalition since PAS' candidates were running on the NF's ticket. However, despite UMNO's hold on the government, PAS managed to influence policy to a certain extent. In a consideration of power-sharing one of the key features to be examined is the extent of this influence. In general terms this also has a bearing on Islam and Islamic *da'wah* (calling to Islam) in Malaysia.

Islamisation

During the period 1974-1977, PAS' role in bringing about change towards a more Islamically-inclined environment was quite clearly evident. This took the form of institutional change as well as the introduction of piecemeal features that benefited Islam. In the economic arena, the significant contribution was the idea of setting up Bank Islam. In the social field all advertisements for alcohol and gambling were taken off the television. Advertisements for the government-run Toto and Social Welfare lotteries were also withdrawn, although these evils were not banned altogether. In addition the practice of serving alcohol at all government and state functions such as banquets also ceased. On another front da'wah work was given a boost with the introduction of the '*da'wah* month', in which all over the country da'wah activities were held in earnest. This event was of special significance because the Islamic resurgence was beginning to be felt and the Islamic tide was beginning to sweep the country.

The then Law Minister, Abdul Kadir Yusof, promised to have the constitution amended to bring it into line with Islam. Besides this *adhah* (call to prayer) was introduced over the government-controlled media. In education the government, under PAS pressure, was forced to set up many institutions for Islamic education, prominent amongst which was the Islamic Teachers Training College. A senior leader of PAS, Hassan Shukri, was appointed to be the chairman of the Da'wah Foundation. Many of the changes came about through the pressure exerted by PAS through its Youth wing, who would meet with ministers to take action on various aspects of the administration. If a particular matter concerned foreign policy, the minister concerned would be approached to take the appropriate action. Similarly, other ministers would be asked by the Youth wing to take the necessary action to bring about changes towards Islam. Of course not every request was entertained, but over the years at least cosmetic change was effected as part of the UMNO's overall strategy to accommodate PAS in order to keep it tied down in the coalition. An important development in foreign affairs was the move taken to bring Malaysia closer to the other Muslim nations and to give greater prominence to these countries.

Achievements and Failures

Besides seeing external changes in society towards a more Islamic environment PAS also benefited in other terms. Though the political climate had cooled considerably since the pre-69 situation of keen UMNO / PAS rivalry and its effects especially on the rural population, yet such calmness did not mean the demise of PAS' continued acceptance by the people. On the contrary, *da'wah* activities carried on in the rural areas (especially the FELDA schemes), and PAS' growing influence in these schemes alarmed UMNO. More people came forward to become members as there was nothing to fear since PAS itself was a part of the government. This period saw an influx of government officers into PAS, a considerable number of whom were university lecturers. They saw a better Islamic alternative in PAS. A very significant development was the introduction of PAS influence into traditional UMNO strongholds, a situation that caused many crossovers to PAS. UMNO leaders became further alarmed and pressed for a verbal understanding that there should be no crossovers in future. The general non-suppression of PAS activities was conducive to its rapid expansion into many areas of the peninsula.

This period, however, did not bring anything really significant in terms of structural change, as was mentioned earlier. Before enticing PAS to join the coalition, UMNO praised Islam and agreed verbally to give the widest possible latitude for PAS to promote Islam in the administration and in the country, yet later the most basic demand of changing the constitution was ignored by UMNO. The changes brought so far were not substantial because it was never UMNO's intention to implement Islam. Policy changes really did not take shape. Although UMNO tried to project an outward appearance of favouring changes in policy this was merely propagandist in nature.

On the part of PAS, besides the general guiding principle put forward to the government for the implementation of Islam, there was no detailed comprehensive blueprint prepared. The basis for power-sharing as was said earlier was primarily for preserving Malay-Muslim dominance in the face of the non-Muslim challenge. Despite this PAS efforts could have succeeded if UMNO had been sincere, because government institutions and machinery in general could have been utilised for preparing the blueprint for administrative reform in the direction of Islamic government. The fact was that UMNO was determined to preserve the existing secular system. This could further be observed from UMNO's hypocrisy, as out of a total of 20 ministries only two were allotted to PAS, and even these were not leading ministries in the government. The question of PAS' guiding policy for all the ministries, with only two in hand, did not arise at all. Thus PAS was relegated to 'advising' and 'pressurising' the government on an ad-hoc basis.

Overall achievement was mixed, however the trends towards Islam in society became more pronounced from time to time. PAS' expansion into traditional UMNO areas caused much anxiety among UMNO leaders. On the other hand PAS felt betrayed because UMNO had reneged on its promise to make structural changes, it therefore stepped uppressure on the government to take bolder steps. UMNO would have none of it and in the ensuing process expelled PAS from the coalition.

Out of the Coalition

The removal of PAS did not happen immediately, it took place after quite a standoff. UMNO had expected PAS to leave the coalition, and PAS knew it would only be a matter of time before it would be removed. The PAS leadership did not want to make the first move, since this could be interpreted negatively by the people — PAS could be blamed for causing Malay - Muslim disunity. If instead it were expelled then UMNO would be held responsible. Unfortunately due to the fact that the Malays are not issue-oriented and were too reliant on the UMNO-controlled media, the expulsion of PAS did not become an issue and there was little benefit from it.

The removal of PAS from the ruling coalition was not the end of the matter. PAS left the NF government with an expanded influence amongst the people, especially the Muslims. As far as UMNO was concerned, after failing in its effort to curtail PAS' influence whilst in the coalition, it would now pursue more relentlessly its efforts to destroy PAS, since the party was now outside the government and was free to act as it wished outwith the constraints of government. The primary strategy was to weaken PAS' traditional hold in the east coast, especially in the state of Kelantan. Besides this UMNO was fully aware that though more people had joined PAS, the party was still in a dilemma since it had been in government and thus could not simply dismiss the government as not having Islamic tendencies. Once outside, PAS' initial problem was how best to explain that the experiment had failed.

UMNO tried hard to undermine PAS and Kelantan was targeted as the starting point to begin its activities. In 1977, the NF government caused disturbances in the state. Emergency rule was proclaimed and this opportunity was taken to attack PAS from all angles. The hardship faced by the people was blamed on PAS though the federal government had continued to practise discrimination against the state. As mentioned above PAS' campaign strategy was badly affected as a result of its having been a government - component party. Seeing PAS in trouble, the Sultan of the state who sided with the NF, called an election in 1978. PAS was thrashed out of the 19 seats held previously and only managed to keep two. In Terengganu it lost all nine seats that it had held and in Kedah it only managed to keep a paltry two seats.

The election of 1978 once again put PAS' strategy into question and its power-sharing experience was thoroughly re-examined. Though it lost badly in the elections, if this is any measure of its strength, the experience was very valuable for at least one reason. The decision to participate in a coalition came at a time when the Islamic resurgence was just beginning and thus PAS needed to gauge the sentiments of the Muslims, of a movement committed towards Islam working 'from inside'. It was also useful in that it proved the theory that 'working from inside' (power-sharing) is fraught with disaster unless certain conditions are met. These we will now examine.

Basis for Power-Sharing

In deciding the mechanics of power-sharing, an Islamic movement may have to consider two very basic principles. PAS feels that these principles are necessary to guide the strategy of working from within the system or even when any Islamic movement succeeds in forming a government through forging a coalition with others. First, in any coalition, the Islamic movement or *jama'ah* concerned must be the party to decide on policy and therefore be in a position to set the objective of power-sharing in such a way that it would play the primary role in any government. The second principle is that it must never be forced into implementing policies already decided upon by others. As part of the power-sharing set-up they must not be made to merely implement the policy. In short the Islamic movement must be the policy-maker.

Unfortunately PAS' experience of 1972-1977 and especially 1974-1977 did not live up to the second of the principles described above. In the context of parliamentary democracy, the Islamic movement, based on to PAS' experience, must make use of the opportunity it has because it still remains in the domain of *muwajaha silmiyah* (opposition in an open peaceful manner). Power-sharing would still be possible as long as the conditions for *muwajaha silmiyah* continue to exist, otherwise it could not possibly be carried out.

The general erosion of PAS influence following the 1978 debacle was in fact a blessing in disguise. The period immediately following 1978 was one of reconstruction. A significant development in the post 1978 era was that structural changes in PAS were taking place, especially at top leadership level. With the Islamic resurgence at its peak and the victory of the Islamic revolution of Iran, PAS members moved for a change in leadership. Thus in 1981-83 the leadership of the *ulema* came to be firmly entrenched.

This change in the leadership also brought about a set of new guiding principles that gave PAS a shot in the arm, and in the ensuing years raised PAS back to its former status as the premier party and movement struggling for the cause of Islam in Malaysia.

The main principle was that the top leadership must be in a position to understand Islam from its original source and be able to interpret it in the light of present day political processes and developments, whilst maintaining its pristine purity. Such interpretations in other words must in no way deviate from the established principles of Islam. Expediency can never forsake principles. Other secondary principles include the integrity of the leadership which must be shown in their modest way of life and high level of sacrifice for the cause of Islam.

The Second Coalition

The second power-sharing experience for PAS was in 1990. UMNO had undergone a major split when fierce internal struggles caused the original party to become null and void as a result of a court decision. Following this sudden demise and the failure of several leaders and followers of the old UMNO to revive it through the courts, the Spirit of 46 — more commonly known as the Semangat 46 — came into being. The primary aim of this UMNO splinter-group was to continue the struggle to revive the old UMNO and destroy the new UMNO that had been formed in its place. The Semangat continued to enjoy pockets of support despite a relentless campaign to discredit it by the new UMNO led by the Prime Minister, Mahathir. In the 1990 general election, PAS regained Kelantan with the help of Semangat as well as two other small Muslim parties - Berjsa and Hamim. The coalition, which was aptly named the Ummah Solidarity Movement (Angkatan Perpaduan Ummah) won all the 39 state seats. In Terengganu the coalition managed to lessen the NF's influence by taking ten seats. This victory was all the more important considering the nature of these two states, which are the most populous Muslim areas of the country.

During the last two years, power-sharing with the Semangat has been very satisfactory. The nature of power-sharing in this case differs radically from the first experience, in that it is PAS that is deciding on policy matters, which has given the Islamic movement a tremendous boost. In Kelantan, PAS hold 24 seats, the Semangat 11, the NF two, with Berjasa and Hamim holding one each. While the coalition led by PAS wrested all 39 seats in the October 1990 elections, the new UMNO forced the courts to declare two candidates as non-Semangat members through back-door tactics, thus giving the NF two seats by default. However, this slight setback has not in any way hindered the PAS-based coalition government from implementing the policies it has set forth.

The power-sharing concept applied in the case of the present government of Kelantan falls within the scope of the first principle of power-sharing described above. In this case PAS clearly decides on policy, following which the coalition implements these policies. The past two years bear witness to the development. As a matter of fact the Semangat has been very cooperative and is beginning to understand the objectives of an Islamic administration. Despite this, PAS believes that it can go it alone if at any point the Semangat decides to leave the coalition. Power will still remain with PAS because of its majority in the State Assembly.

Coalition in Kelantan

PAS-led rule in Kelantan over the past two years has been very positive for the development of Islam in that state as an Islamic-based government is now in power. The stress on Islam in all matters pertaining to the state has even caused the neighbouring state of Terengganu, which is in NF hands, to acknowledge the importance of Islam as a guiding factor in administrative matters. One of the successes of the Kelantan government is the abolition of gambling and alcohol. Also all the extravaganza associated with the previous NF regime has been done away with. Despite an all-out economic blockade by the Federal government, Kelantan has managed to develop economically, albeit quite slowly.

The strength of the Kelantan government lies in its Islamic base and in a leadership which is totally committed to Islam. Seeing it grow from strength to strength, the NF have tried to woo it into some form of coalition, but this was rejected outright because it would not fit a concept of power-sharing that would be in line with Islamic principles. After attaining power PAS' objective is to make Kelantan a model Islamic government fully aware of the constraint and limitation it has to face. Many of thc measures taken by the Kelantan government have been very well received not only by the Kelantanese, but have also acknowledged by people in other states.

In fact some of these measures have also been emulated by the Federal Government, for example, the cessation of the practice of presenting token mementos to senior officials or ministers upon officiating any ceremony. The abolition of licences for operating gambling outlets was soon copied by the Sarawak state government, but unfortunately the UMNO-controlled Federal government reinstated the operators by issuing them with new licences and then 'demanding' that premises be provided by the State government for such activities. On the whole the PAS-led State government is moving steadily and cautiously towards the full application of Islamic principles in government and society. This also includes the introduction of the *shari'ah*, which is evidenced by the recent proposal to enact hooded laws in the state.

In conclusion, the Islamic movement must participate dynamically in different situations with the firm purpose of establishing Islam. Before deciding on participating in any power set-up certain preconditions must be met. The prevailing political climate is a very important condition for the Islamic movement's participation in active politics. By active politics we mean the utilisation of political processes conducive to the Islamic movement. In this case in any given country, we must examine the existing political system to gauge the extent of our possible participation. For example, in a country like Malaysia which practises a limited form of democracy, the political process of elections can be a vehicle for the further propagation of Islam as well as allowing the Islamic movement to attain a certain position that would allow it to either share power, threaten the status quo or seize limited power outright.

The process of elections should rightly be seen as a mechanism for the Islamic movement to get the Islamic message across to the masses as well as an opportunity to forge a power-base. In the case of Malaysia again, the concept of Federalism as is practised now cannot possibly rule out the development of a series of Islamic states falling one after another to the Islamic movement. All this may happen against a background of 'democracy' or limited democracy which calls for the implementation of the approach of '*muwajaha silmiyah*', whereas *muwajaha bil-quwwah* (confrontation siththe use of force) will come about naturally if political conditions change, as for example with the end of such a limited form of democracy. Thus, in spite of such things as the present stringent control of the media, to call for a revolution at this juncture in the Malaysian context would not be wise and would be against the grain of political development.

Conclusion

We believe that no secular regime will allow for the flourishing of the Islamic movement in any form, whether in or out of power. We also believe that when the forces of Islam reach certain heights in their struggle then these secular forces will definitely act to destroy their power. No secular regime has yet accommodated the Islamic movement in real terms and has always shown its oppressive face, only the degree of oppression varies from country to country. We believe too that the masses must not only be told of oppression but must bear witness to it. In time to come such oppression will be experienced and when that happens the legitimate Islamic aspirations of the Muslim *ummah* will take their due course.

POWER-SHARING ISLAM

FAILURES

This chapter consists of papers that discuss several unsuccessful experiments of power-sharing. They tell the stories of aborted democratic processes in Algeria, Afghanistan and Egypt. Several other locations in the Muslim World not discussed here, such as Tunisia and Tajekistan, have succumbed to the same fate.

The first paper in this chapter is by Anwar Haddam who discusses the Algerian Islamic Movement's Experience in relation with the new World Order. The paper includes an outline of the political agenda of the Islamic Salvation Front (FIS).

The second paper, which also discusses the Algerian experience, is contributed by Rachid Ben Eissa who holds the West partly responsible for the failure of the Algerian democratic process.

The Third paper is presented by an Afghanistan affairs expert, Kamal El-Helbawi, who accounts for the various Afghan factions involved in the current struggle for power and underlines the local and international factors that contribute to the persistance of the current crisis.

Finally, in a paper entitled "The Future of Power-Sharing in Egypt", Dr. Essam Al-Erian describes the current Egyptian political situation and the experience of the Islamic Movement in Egypt's short-lived democracy.

THE POLITICAL EXPERIMENT OF THE ALGERIAN ISLAMIC MOVEMENT AND THE NEW WORLD ORDER

Anwar N. Haddam

'Thereafter We set you on the right Guidance (the Shari'a) so follow it, and do not follow the desires of those who know not.'

(Qur'an 45:18)

Introduction

The profound and comprehensive changes that are affecting the world as a whole may be described as the appearance and establishment of a New World Order. In the aftermath of the disintegration of the communist block, many people in the world have realised that security and the commitment to a stable peace are no longer simply local or regional phenomena. They are global issues that impact on the entire world body.

The issue of human rights was proclaimed decades ago in a United Nations resolution, but it is only more recently that most nations of the world have come to see its importance as an unequivocal and undeniable right and as a prerequisite to good relations between countries. However, the ideal of providing and protecting collective as well as individual human rights for all, is far from being realised in many countries of the world.

As humanity is progressing in its civilizational development and technological advancement, the world's economy has evolved from being country-based to being world-based. Today, nations understand that global stability and good international relations cannot be achieved without effective economic prosperity.

Although humanity has experimented with many different approaches to addressing the above issues, namely the issues of global security, respect for human rights, and economic prosperity, it has only recently reached a near consensus on how to achieve these goals. Political pluralism as a way for people to govern themselves is being recognised by most nations of the world as the way to achieve these aims, since it is the most efficient way to safeguard against tyranny, despotism, and dictatorship.

In order to reach the exercise of a mature and responsible political pluralism, people in different parts of the world have had to go through various self-improving stages. In this regard Allah says in the Qur'an: "Never will Allah change the condition of a people until they change what is in themselves." (13:11)

The struggle of the Algerians to rid themselves of French colonialism in the 1950's inspired colonised people around the world. In December 1991, Algerians set a different kind of example, successfully completing the first round of the most democratic elections ever held in North Africa. However, the Islamic Front for Salvation (FIS), a political party which has emerged from the people of Algeria as an expression of their identity and aspirations, is being unfairly denied its victory at the polls.

Mr. Edward P. Djerejian, the US Assistant Secretary of State, Bureau of Near East and South Asian Affairs, said on June 4th 1992 at Meridian House, "Those who are prepared to take specific steps toward free elections, creating independent judiciaries, promoting the rule of law, reducing restrictions on the press, respecting the rights of minorities, and guaranteeing individual rights, will find us ready to recognise and support their efforts".

The FIS recognises and adheres to the above principles of global security, respect for human rights, and economic prosperity through free enterprise dynamism in non strategic sectors. It intends, once in power, to implement these concepts and build its relations with other nations on the basis of these principles.

This paper is devoted to the FIS' political experiment in terms of its contribution to the establishment of the New World Order. The first section will be a brief review of the Algerian history; the second section will address the political situation in Algeria in the recent years. The third and last section will be devoted to the political struggle of the FIS against the corrupt Algerian establishment, to bring about a positive change.

ALGERIA:
The Rise of an Islamic State — A Journey Through Time

Forty years after the death of Prophet Mohammed (peace be upon him), Islam reached the people of North Africa. The new converts to Islam carried the flame of enlightenment across the Mediterranean sea to bring the call of Islam to new people. For centuries Andalusia stood as a testimony to the creative genius of the Muslims. From the 15th to the early 19th centuries, Muslims in North Africa stood up to the church-backed European regimes who were increasingly eager to colonise and exploit Muslim lands and resources.

Then in 1830 France invaded Algeria and subjugated its people. A brutal military rule was implemented, and economic disparity drove the people to starvation. The ultimate aim of the French was to destroy the Islamic identity of the Algerians, who almost became 'European. However, North African Muslims never surrendered. Ameer Abdulkadir, Sheikh Al Mokrani, Sheikh Bou Amama and other Muslim scholars waged a continuous *jihad* against the French oppressors.

In 1930, as France celebrated the 100th anniversary of its Algerian occupation, the *jamiat al-ulamaa al-muslimeen* (Association of Algerian Muslim Scholars) headed by Sheikh Abdal-Hameed Ibnu Badis, embarked on the vital mission of reviving the faith and cultural identity of the Algerian people.

In 1954, the National Liberation Front (FLN) was formed. It was headed by Al-Arbi Ibn Mehidi, Youssef Zighout, Colonel Armirouche, Mustapha Ben Boulaid and Abassi Madani (the FIS president) who declared jihad against the forces of occupation. The initial goal of the historic FLN leaders as proclaimed in their declaration, was the 'restoration of the independent Algerian state within the framework of Islamic principles'. The French military reaction was very brutal, especially against the civilian population. In 1962, after a seven year war that left a million and a half martyrs, the struggle of the Algerian people culminated in the accession to independence.

Following independence, a group of military officers headed by Boumediene installed Ben Bella as head of the Algerian government. Socialism and one party rule were imposed. Ben Bella consolidated his power by eliminating anyone opposed to his regime. He was responsible for banning *jamiat al-ulamaa Al-muslimeen*, and jailing the elderly Sheikh Al-Basheer Al-Ibrahimi. In June 1965, Colonel Boumediene seized power and put Ben Bella under arrest. He also banned *jamiat al-qiyam* (the Association of Values), which was a newly formed association of Muslim scholars, and an extension to *jamiat al-ulamaa*, and that counted among its notable founders, Sheikh Ahmad Sahnoun, and Sheikh Abassi Madani. Boumediene's era had also seen the beginning of the disastrous period of industrialisation, engincered by Belaid Abdessalem and Ahmad Ghozali, who were then the economy minister and the chairman of the powerful oil company Sonatrach. These two men were the ones who were later called upon by the military junta to serve as prime ministers after the coup d'etat of January 11th 1992.

In 1978, after Boumediene's death, colonel Chadli was selected to replace him. During this period of authoritarian rule, and despite the banning of *jamiat al-ulamaa* and *jamiat al-qiyam*, mosques in general, and students' mosques in university campuses in particular, remained the only bastions of opposition to successive dictators.

Under successive military regimes, Algerians experienced economic and social hardship. Algeria's external debt reached $27 billion, causing a rapid decline in the standard of living. Meanwhile, a cast of privileged people were becoming defiantly and openly richer. Deteriorating standards of living and lack of freedom sparked the events of October 1988. For about a week, tens of thousands of Algerian youths marched angrily demanding justice and equity, and attacking all the symbols of the establishment; symbols of injustice and despotism. The regime responded by resorting to military repression resulting in at least 500 deaths and 1,000 arrests. When the use of force proved unsuccessful, President Chadli was compelled to initiate a process leading to a multi-party system in an attempt to quell public anger, and diffuse the crisis.

The Political Situation in Algeria: October 1988 - December 1991

The political developments in Algeria, from the tragic events of October 1988 until the historic date of December 26th 1991, could be summarised as follows:

The Algerian people realised that no real transformation of society could occur without amending the constitution. Indeed, a crucial memorandum was signed and submitted to President Chadli by Sheikh A. Sahnoun, head of *rabitat ad-dawaa al-islamiyah* (the Islamic League of Dawaa), on behalf of the Algerian Islamic Movement. That memorandum suggested ways to diffuse the multidimensional crisis facing Algeria, through the promotion of the rule of law, the separation between the executive, legislative and judiciary bodies, the encouragement of free enterprise, the authorisation of freedom of the press, the freedom to form political parties, and the organisation of free elections at all levels. In fact under pressure from the Algerian people, the constitution was amended in February 1986. The most important amendment was that the new constitution guaranteed the freedom to form political associations. Freedom of the press was also a major breakthrough whose consequences are and will continue to be highly beneficial to the transformation process. It was also realised that a state controlled economy is an obstacle to the growth of economic prosperity. There was a desperate need for better management, as well as for a restructuring of the institutions. The existing weak infrastructure, neglected for decades, was in need of reconstruction. The restructuring of a society to make it more ethical and more productive is of such importance that no other reform in any sector of life can succeed without it.

Most of these attempts were unsuccessful since the Algerian people lacked legitimately elected representative bodies. On June 12th 1990 and December 26th 1991, the people of Algeria spoke up for themselves and chose first their local government officers and then their representatives in the parliament. These were the first free elections that the country had ever held since its independence in 1962. It was an overwhelming victory for the FIS through the ballot box. This illustrates the political experiment of the Algerian Islamic Movement, and its leadership in bringing the rest of the Muslim world to a harmonious coexistence within a New World Order.

President Richard Nixon said in his book, 'Seize the Moment' (published September 1992), "Fundamentalists can fill the streets in the Muslim world with vocal demonstrations, but they cannot yet take power through the polls." The Algerian experience however has proved that it is possible for an Islamic movement to take power through the polls, and hence to be capable of establishing a strong and stable state. The question now is whether the West is ready to accept this reality: Islam, at the state level, is back. Indeed the Algerian experiment is a decisive test for the West — will it honour its principles of human rights and freedom of choice for all peoples, and hence pave the way for the rest of the Muslim world to follow the Algerian example, or will it ignore the aspiration of the Muslim peoples to recover their identity, and hence build a new Iron Curtain between the two civilisations? Certainly, the West's continuous support for and condoning of dictatorial regimes will not help in establishing a world of justice and peace.

The FIS and the Political Struggle for Positive Change

The Islamic Front for Salvation is putting forward comprehensive solutions to the ideological, political, economic, social and cultural problems that plague Algeria.

The ideological framework presented by the FIS is based on the fact that Algeria is part of the Islamic Nation. It takes into consideration the political culture of the Algerian society as a whole, part of which is to consider the mosques as the heart of the society, not only gathering the people to worship, but also offering them a forum to express their concerns on all aspects of their daily life. At the same time the FIS does not intend and will not attempt to build a theocratic system in the image of the system experienced by the West for centuries. This was clearly stated by the leader of the Algerian Islamic Movement, the late Sheikh Abdelhamid Ibn Badis, in January 1938 in a paper titled, 'The Basis of Governorship in Islam':

"No one has the right to manage the affairs of the people without their consent. It is incumbent on the people to delegate power or to take it away."

He also said in the same paper, promoting the rule of law:

"The people will not be governed except by the law that they chose and knew the benefits of for themselves. Therefore they obey the law because it is their own law, not because it is imposed on them by any other authority, be it an individual or a group."

He continued by promoting the multi-party system:

"The people reserve the right to discuss their affairs with those in position to hold them accountable for their actions and to make sure that they follow the choice of the society, not their own."

So, by establishing a political party, namely the FIS, the Algerian Islamic Movement opts for honest competition through the people's choice. The FIS has advocated the principle of respecting the will of the Algerian people, as expressed through the ballot box.

The political programme of the FIS aims at institutionalising a stable governing system, a system which has to be representative of the Algerian society in its plurality. The means to achieve this is through political pluralism that fully guarantees, implements and preserves minority rights. Sheikh Abassi Madani, the president and the spokesman of the FIS, repeatedly stated that one cannot conceive a strong and stable state without guaranteeing a free political opposition.

The FIS economic programme is based on the principle of economic growth. The world has recognised that economy has passed the stage of centralisation and central state monopoly. But it should also realise that a totally free market economy neither serve nor preserve the strategic interests of sovereign nations. The attraction of capital to revitalise the economy is seen as a necessary measure, since the FIS foresees participation in the global economy as a necessary building block of any country's economy. However, at the same time, the relations among states and among institutions are to be built on a partnership basis to avoid over-exploitation, and to guarantee proper and sound management of human as well as material resources. The FIS will honour payment of all debts which have been truly used for economic development. However, any future FIS-led government will not recognise any debt received by the junta who seized power through the military coup d'etat on 11 January 1992.

The FIS bases its social programme on the principle that man is the main axis of the universe, and the author of civilisations. The FIS aims at building a balanced society where the rights to life, health, welfare, and education at all levels for all components of society are guaranteed. The FIS has envisioned its programme based on the fact that the Algerian society is family-oriented, and on the principle that men and women are to be granted the same status. The separation into classes is to be avoided and abolished by all possible means. The late Malek Bennabi, another great leader and thinker of the Algerian Islamic Movement stated in his book, 'Conditions for the Renaissance': "The problem is neither a problem of men nor of women, but rather a problem of society as a whole."

To sum up, the FIS endeavors to address all social problems in a comprehensive, scientific, and balanced way.

The cultural programme put forward by the FIS relies on the concept of the coexistence of civilisations. It aims at the preservation of the cultural and historical traditions of the Algerian society, as these constitute essential elements of its identity. The rehabilitation of science is of paramount importance, for a society without a good educational and scientific system cannot aim at any effective prosperity.

With regard to international relations and diplomacy, the FIS bases its approach on moderation and equity in addressing world problems. The FIS unequivocally supports all oppressed people and considers the issue of human rights, collective as well as individual, as a guiding principle for foreign relations. Honouring treaties with regional and international bodies (concluded prior to the January 1992 coup d'etat), which respect the strategic and national interests of the Algerian people is seen by the FIS as a necessity, since complex geopolitical and economic ties necessitate involvement on the world scene.

The above is a brief summary of the programme the Algerian Islamic Movement proposed to the Algerian people through its political mouthpiece, the FIS. This programme is the fruit of hard and in-depth work carried out by the Movement far from the spotlight over more than six decades.

Local Government Experiment:

Fully confident in its Islamic ideals, the FIS bases its policy on ideological challenges and peaceful persuasion rather than the forceful imposition of ideas. These ideals have been the practised policy of the FIS since its inception. Since the overwhelming victory of FIS in the municipal (local government) elections of June 1990, in which a large number of highly-educated FIS candidates were elected to office, it has demonstrated its ability to strive to improve the living conditions of the population. These efforts were initially hampered by the central government, who deprived local governments of many of their previous prerogatives, and cut their budgets in an effort to undermine their popularity. However, the population enthusiastically supported the local governments with voluntary assistance and additional taxes

It is this restoration of confidence and trust between the local governments and their constituencies that won the FIS the full support of the majority of Algerians, as shown by the landslide victory in the first round of parliamentary elections held on 26 December 1992.

Parliamentary Elections:

After several delays in the parliamentary elections, which due to public pressure, were scheduled to be held in June 1991, the rulers in Algeria decreed a new electoral law designed to give the ruling party (FLN) an edge over all other parties. This law was judged unfair, and thus was challenged by all other major parties.

After the failure by all political means to enforce a change in the unjust electoral law, the FIS called for a political strike and peaceful demonstrations at the end of May 1991. Despite the constitutional legality of such protests, the regime responded with repressive means. President Chadli dissolved the government and declared a State of Emergency. Sheikh Abassi Madani, the FIS president and his deputy Sheikh Ali Belhadj, along with five other FIS leaders were arrested. The regime also carried out a broad-based campaign of arrests aimed at undermining the FIS' solid and widespread popular support. According to the Algerian League for the Defence of Human Rights, three hundred people were killed, eight thousand were arrested, and twelve thousand FIS sympathisers were dismissed from their jobs.

Despite the conspiracy against it and the open hostilities from the regime which deprived it of its top leaders, the FIS' response was strikingly balanced and responsible. A communique co-signed by Sheikh Mohammed Said, a leading member of the Algerian Islamic movement and spokesman of the Islamic League of Da'wah and by Abdelkader Hachani, member of FIS' Consultative Council issued on July 2nd 1992, reads:

"Once more the Algerian governmenthas shown its usual antipathy to political opposition in general and to the Islamic movement in particular,a movement which represents the aspirations of the Algerian people. This movement has embarked on a project aimed at the implementation of Islam as a global answer to societal problems.

The response of the government to the ideals and demands of the Algerian people was brutal repression, effected by murder, detention, damage to property, destruction of houses of worship, terrorisation of the civilian population and the systematic destruction of the FIS party organs and its headquarters. In line with the political status and agenda of the FIS as a genuine representative of the aspirations and ideals of the Algerian people which strives to harness and mobilise committed and sincere human resources for the sake of fulfilling the Islamic project in accordance with political rules, we stress the following:

In the last meeting with Sheikh Abassi Madani, prior to his arrest, he insisted on preserving the FIS as a political party endorsing a global solution, whose vindication will be put forward openly and in the context of the law...

To conclude we call upon the people to remain steadfast and be patient... Darkness, no matter how long it lasts, will give way to the dawn of justice."

Sheikh Mohammed Said was arrested a week later, in his capacity as the new interim FIS spokesman, in the middle of a press conference with national and international news media.

After more than five months of emergency law and detentions of the FIS leadership, the government decided to revise the unfair electoral law, and reschedule the two-round parliamentary elections. Moreover the Ghozali-led government repeatedly promised fair elections and stated that it would abide by the results of the polls, regardless of the participation rate.

On 26 December 1991 Algerians went to the ballot box to choose their parliamentary representatives. Of the 430 seats contested by some 50 political parties and a number of independent candidates, 207 were decided in the first round. The FIS won 188, the FFS (the Front of Socialist Forces) 25, the ruling FLN (the National Liberation Front) won 16 seats and three seats went to independent candidates.

On January 11th 1992, the military seized power and announced the cancellation of the second round of elections, which were to take place five days later. Algerians were denied their inalienable right to freely elect their legitimate government, merely because they preferred an Islamic state, a state of truth and justice, over dictatorship and puppet regimes.

In a move to contain popular anger, Mohammed Boudiaf, the so-called historical father of the freedom struggle against French colonialism, was called upon to head the 'High Council of State' after a self-imposed exile of 27 years in Morocco. In a dramatic move, the High Council of State declared a year-long State of Emergency, banned the FIS, arrested its interim president, Abdelkader Hachani, and curtailed the freedom of press. Concentration camps were set-up throughout the Sahara desert to detain many thousands of FIS members and sympathisers.

The arrival of Mohammed Boudiaf to head the HCS was praised and advertised by political analysts as a symbol of honesty. He was considered to be the only person who could bring back justice and harmony to Algeria. However, it soon became apparent that his assault on certain segments of the society was politically motivated and a certain recipe for disaster. On June 29th 1992, Boudiaf was killed by his own bodyguard.

The army then picked Colonel Ali Kafi to head the HCS and Belaid Abdessalem to form a new government. As both of them had been 'barons' of the regime since 1962, these nominations were a clear sign of the return to the dark era of one party rule, and despotic government.

The Aftermath

More than a year after the military coup d'etat of January 1992, allegedly carried out for the sake of saving democracy, the state's economy is in a free fall, and the country does not produce even the vital minimum required for its survival.

The agricultural sector is still unable to generate enough to meet the people's demands. Oil revenues are directed towards the refunding of foreign debt, accumulated during years of corrupt governments, and towards financing imports for immediate consumption. The country is still far from having a real monetary policy, which would be the only solution to offset the huge amount of Algerian currency which has been distributed by the regime since 1962, without any real economic counterpart value. This situation is leading Algeria towards dramatic hyper-inflation in the 'Russian style'. The regime is only hastening the unprecedented economic catastrophe towards which the country is heading by injecting liquidates into the economic field from time to time without the slightest precaution.

In trying to wipe out its latest defeat, the present illegitimate regime foolishly attempted to discredit the FIS in the eyes of the world. After having orchestrated the tragic bombing of Algiers Airport, where many Algerian civilians were killed, the regime in power ascribed it to the current leaders of the FIS, Sheikh Mohammed Said, Abderezak Rejjame and Yakhlef Cherrati, in flagrant violation of both the penal code procedure and the information code. They resorted to a televised 'confession' by one of the elected members of parliament, who had been tortured until close to death. This kind of action, reminiscent of Stalin's era, can never be accepted as the behaviour of a 'State of Law'.

Conclusions

The FIS considers the freedom to express views, the freedom to form political parties, and the freedom to hold elections as prerequisites to the achievement of its unique and genuine solution to the multi-dimensional crisis from which Algeria is suffering. What should be explained to the western world is that Islam is the foundation of Algerian society, and that the FIS is its expression. The FIS' success is a mere expression of the wish of the people to recover their historical, and cultural identity through a real transformation of their society. The Algerians should not to be portrayed as a symbol against western interests. Historically, western nations have had better relations with freely elected rulers than with imposed military dictatorships. Stability of government, reconstruction of the economy and the transformation of society cannot be brought about if the free choice of the people is ignored. The New World Order, proposed by the West after the collapse of the communist block, cannot be credible if it ignores the identity of any of the world's peoples.

The Algerian odyssey will undoubtedly have considerable repercussions in the upsurging Muslim world. The positive nature of future relations between the Muslim world and the West's proposed New World Order is very much tied to the success of the FIS enterprise and to the positive attitude of the western world towards it.

Allaj says in the Holy Qur'an: "Say, O People of the Scriptures, come to a common word between ourselves and yourselves."

THE ALGERIAN EXPERIMENT

Rachid Ben Eissa

Prior to discussing the Algerian experiment, it should be stressed that one cannot discuss any Muslim experiment today without referring to the prevailing international situation. In his paper, Professor Gellner has pointed out the two big events that have occurred this century - the demise of communism and the rise of Islam. From a Muslim perspective I believe that now the West has overcome its schism - the Marxist schism - it has never been as strong as it is today. In contrast, the Muslim community has never been so weak as it is today, and the gap between them has never been wider. Until the eighteenth century all societies were developing at more or less the same pace. Today there is no developed Muslim country. I agree we do not go to paradise because of GNP, but the problem is one of survival here and now. We are absent from the nuclear club and the industrial club. We are absent from all serious clubs that are worthy of membership. These are the facts that must be recognised when we talk about power-sharing or power-taking. The survival of the Muslim community is threatened. We face a systematic enterprise to suppress Muslims - we face a media war, we face separatism, we face negation.

If we wish to talk about power-sharing, we can cite some experiments: Indonesia, Egypt, Tunisia, Morocco, Jordan, and Turkey - all in my opinion are failures. Unfortunately all movements which tried to share power were used to legitimise power for others. They were used by their opponents. There remain two experiments, Iran and Sudan, but they do not illustrate the sharing of power; as they simply took power and monopolised it.

Another experiment is Algeria. It has been a unique experience and the most convincing proof of the war the West has opened on us. In Algeria we agreed to play the democratic game. Algeria is the most open of Muslim countries, its people read thousands of copies of le Monde and listen to French radio. A legally-recognised Islamic party participated in the elections and obtained about 80 percent of the votes. All the Western media speaks about is FIS - but what is FIS? It is the people who made FIS king by voting for it.

I no longer believe in the word you are using here - democracy - I really don't know what it is. In Algeria I saw the military take power from the elected party. I saw the Western countries condemn the coup very smoothly but then give money. This week our prime minister is in Paris to get seven billion from France while the media accuses FIS of being an agent of France ! We are agents of France but money goes to the ruling military regime in Algeria ! So it would appear that 'democracy' is good for Western people but it is not valid for Muslims. If Muslims decide that they want their faith to be taken into account when devising their cultural, economic and educational policies, then their party is criminalised and abolished.

In the nineteenth century the West was interfering to protect minorities in the Middle East. Now it is interfering to protect ideological minorities - the Communists who are anti-Muslim and represent less than one percent of the population, but who are given power. The French newspaper in Algeria belongs to Communists. Communists are a tiny minority but they have much media power. The West is there, in our midst, in our television, interfering every day in our politics.

Even in Bosnia it is the same thing. The Muslims there took the majority by vote. They are now suppressed and the West is looking on, explaining why it cannot intervene. When it was Iraq they were anxious to find reasons for intervening, now they are anxious to find reasons for not intervening. They had planes for Baghdad, but they do not have planes for Belgrade. For that reason Algeria, the most westernised of countries knows the West better. They know of Western interference and lies, which is why they are becoming more radicalised.

There are two interlinked demands in the Muslim world. First Muslims want their own identity - they want to assert themselves, to feel that they are Muslims, to be told they are Muslims, to see everything devisedwithin the context of Islam. This claim is a very serious and legitimate one. They want everything to be within the *shari'ah*. But there is another demand. They need development. Their universities do not function well. Their hospitals do not work. We are here in the West to seek political asylum because there is dictatorship. We come here to seek jobs because there is underdevelopment. As I mentioned in the outset, the development gap is now two centuries old. The factors which created these conditions are well known. The important point is that there is no automatic, necessary correlation between *shari'ah* and development. The *shari'ah* was practised in the year one thousand and can be practised now, without development. What is required in a specific, intellectual effort by Muslims to achieve development and normalise Muslim communities like other societies. Development will bring out an Islamic pride in asserting our cultural identity and practice of our faith.

THE FUTURE OF POWER-SHARING IN AFGHANISTAN

Kamal El-Helbawy

During the last twenty years there have been a good number of power-sharing experiments in the Muslim world undertaken in the name of democracy. We see this in Jordan, Lebanon, Malaysia, Kuwait, Turkey, Egypt, Algeria, Tunisia, Morocco, Mauritania, Indonesia, Sudan, Yemen and recently Afghanistan. These experiments have been democratic to varying degrees, but none has been completely democratic.

This process of power-sharing should not be an end in itself in any Muslim country according to the Islamic ideology. It is a means to an end, that is implementation of the divine programme leading to social justice and the full utilisation of efficient human resources for the benefit of humanity at large, not only for Muslim societies.

In the Muslim countries unfortunately the people have very little role to play in administering their countries for many reasons. Among these, state dictatorship, underdevelopment, ignorance, poverty and illiteracy form a high percentage. Consequently the Muslim world in general has had very little role to play in the twentieth century since the fall of the Caliphate of the Ottoman Empire, and we can assume that its role in power-sharing on the international level is not very great, especially in view of the New World Order (or Disorder as it is viewed by many writers and thinkers in different parts of the world.)

The American assumption that the world will always be in need of American leadership leaves no room for power-sharing on an international leadership level, most probably for the rest of this century.

Due to both local and foreign factors, the Muslim world may not be able to reach a peaceful power-sharing system for some years to come. If this is the status quo in most of the Muslim countries at present, it is more serious in Afghanistan in view of 14 years of war that has destroyed almost 70 per cent of the country's infrastructure, 10 per cent of the total population, and left the future of power-sharing very uncertain.

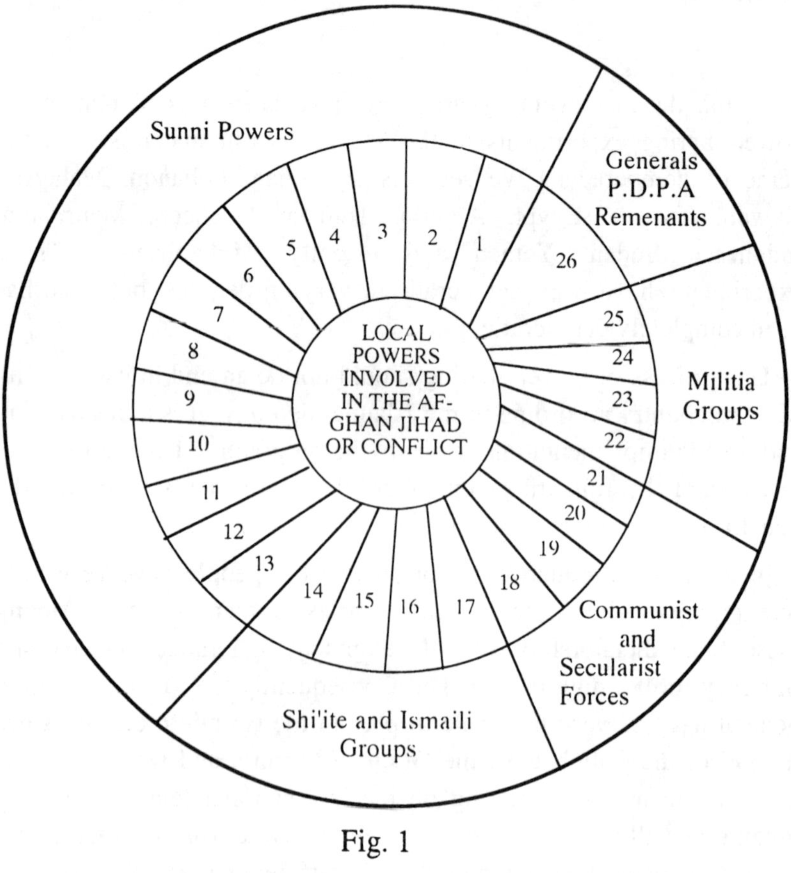

Fig. 1

A. Local Powers

More than 20 powers (the most important ones are shown in Figure 1.)

One of the main problems adding to the present difficulties and challenges in war-torn Afghanistan, is the difficulty of peaceful power-sharing. A quick look at Afghanistan will show us that there are many hands in the pie. The powers affecting the situation in Afghanistan can be divided into the following:

.

First: Sunni Groups:

1. Hizb-e-Islami (Hekmatyar)
2. Jamiat-e-Islami (Rabbani)
3. Ittehad-e-Islami (Sayyaf)
4. Hizb-e-Islami (Khalis)
5. Inqilab-e-Islami (Mohammadi)
6. Mahaz-e-Milli (Gilani)
7. Jabha-e-Nijat-e-Milli (Mujaddedi)

8. Dai-e-Islami,(Qazi Amin Waqad)
(affiliated his small group recently with Hizb-e-Islami, Hekmatyar)
9. Nasrullah Mansoor
(assassinated after he affiliated his small group with Mohammadi)
10. Da'wah Al-Quran Wa Al Sunnah
(The group of Sheikh Jamil ur Rehman Salafi, assassinated two years ago)
11. Field commanders, among them Ahmed Shah Masood, Jalaluddi Haqqani, Abdul Saboor Fareed, Ismail Khan, Abdul Haq and many others who are less famous and less powerful.
12. Tribal leaders (Khans)
13. Tribal leaders (Maulawis)

Second: Shi'ite Groups:

14. Hizb-e-Wahdat Islami (product of merger of nine small Shi'ite parties)
15. Harakat-e-Islami (Mohseni)
16. Shi'ites without fronts
17. Ismailis

Third: Communist and Secularist Forces:

18. Remnants of PDPA (Parcham and Khalq)
19. Shoola-e-Javed. This is a Communist party that was founded and promoted by China to rival other Communist parties promoted by Russia. This party did not participate actively in the war in Afghanistan.
20. Afghan-e-Milli
21. Sittami Milli

Fourth: Militia Groups:

22. Dostum Militia Jouzjani and Jilam Jam
23. Syed Kayan Naderi (Ismaili Militia)
24. Other Sunni independent groups.

Some of these groups are mercenaries.They can be used or purchased by any leader to add to the strength of other groups especially in isolated areas.

Fifth: Generals:

Momen, Tanai, Asif Delawar, Watanjar, Rafi, Gulbazoi, Azeemi, Baba Jan, Kahrman and others. Either they will join different groups or regroup themselves for or against any future power in Kabul. They are a thorn in the path towards peaceful power-sharing.

B. Foreign Powers:

Around 20 groups. The most important ones are shown in figure 2.

I. Super and Ex-Super Powers

1. USA
2. Ex-Soviet Union

II. Regional Powers:

3. India
4. China

III. Muslim Countries:

(5-11) Pakistan, Iran, Saudi Arabia, Egypt, Turkey and all Arab countries were involved in different ways and in different capacities. Some Arab countries were supporting the communists in Afghanistan (Iraq, Southern Yemen, PLO). Some of these powers, particularly: Pakistan, Iran, Saudi Arabia, Egypt and recently Azerbaijan and Tajikistan, still have a role to play in the future of Afghanistan.

IV. Foreign Blocks:

12. NATO
13. Ex-Warsaw Pact

V. European Countries:

14. Western
15. Eastern

VI. International and Regional Organisations:

16. United Nations
17. UN Security Council

VII. Relief Agencies:

18. More than 100 Western relief agencies
19. Around 20 Islamic relief agencies

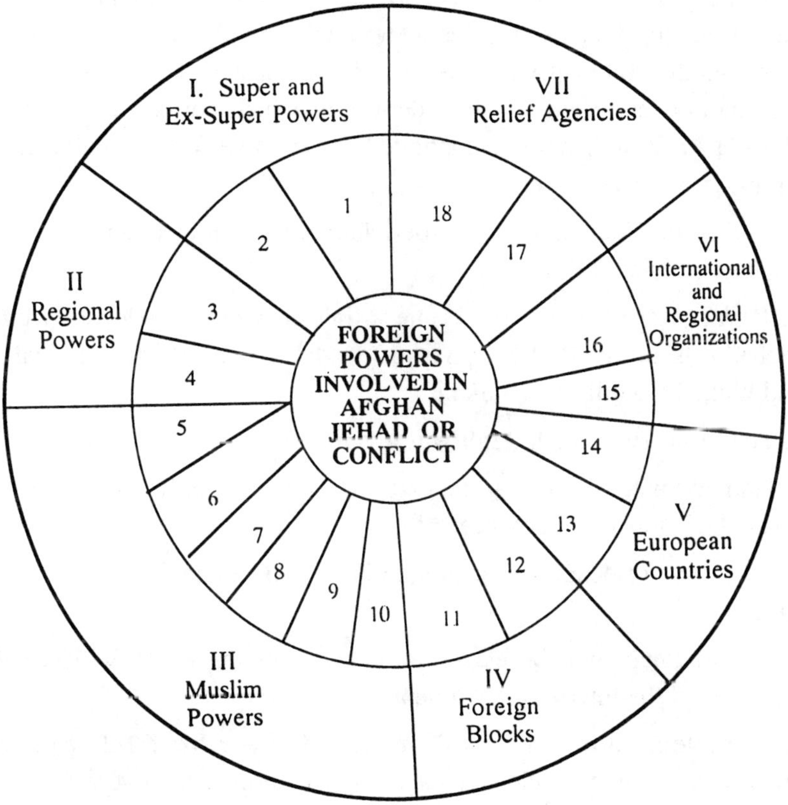

Figure 2

The war in Afghanistan raged for 14 years, starting in 1979 when the Soviets invaded Afghanistan with more than 100,000 troops. Finally the regime of President Najibullah, the last Afghan communist leader, collapsed and he tried to escape on 16 April 1992. At this point the Mujahideen took over power in Kabul in accordance with the Peshawar Accord that stipulated the following:

1. A fifty member council led by Professor Mujaddedi will take over the government after going to Kabul. Professor Mujaddedi will be an acting interim President for two months only. Professor Burhanuddin Rabbani will take over power in Kabul for a period of four months as an interim President after which period, Shura Ahle Hal Wa Aqad (a form of an appointed consultative council) will select a president for 1-1/2 years.

2. Gulbuddin Hekmatyar of Hizb-e-Islam or his nominee will be given the post of Prime Minister.

3. Three assistants to the Prime Minister will be selected from Ittehad-e-Islami of Professor Sayyaf, Hizb-e-Islami of Maulvi Khalis and Ittehad-e-Milli of Pir Gilani.

4. The Ministry of the Interior was given to Engineer Ahmed Shah.

5. Ahmed Shah Masood. of the party of Burhanuddin Rabbani will be given the Ministry of Defence.

6. The party of Maulvi Mohammad Nabi Mohammadi will have the Justice Ministry.

7. A parliament will be elected after two months which will select members of the interim government.

8. The interim government will remain in power for 1-1/2 years to prepare the ground for elections leading to a permanent government.

9. Hekmatyar of Hizb-e-Islami did not participate at the beginning and then nominated Mr. Fareed Abdul Saboor as Prime Minister during Rabbani's four month tenure period.

A government headed by Professor Sibghatullah Mujaddedi was

established in Kabul for two months, then Professor Rabbani took over as an interim President for four months, but the situation was never calm in Kabul for two consecutive weeks. Different warlords have been controlling different areas in and around Kabul since the fall of the Communist regime. The civil war continued until the Islamabad Accord was signed.

THE ISLAMABAD ACCORD

On the 7th.March 1993 the Accord was signed. All the parties and groups concerned have agreed on the following things:

i. Formation of a government for a period of 18 months in which

President Burhanuddin Rabbani would remain President and Engineer Gulbuddin Hekmatyar or his nominee would assume the office of Prime Minister. The powers of the President and Prime Minister and his cabinet which have been formulated through mutual consultations will form part of this Accord.

ii. The Cabinet shall be formed by the Prime Minister in consultations with the President and leaders of Mujahideen parties within two weeks of the signing of this Accord.

iii. The following electoral process is agreed for implementation in a period of not more than 18 months with effect from December 29th 1992:

a. The immediate formation of an independent Election Commission by all parties with full powers.

b. The Election Commission will be mandated to hold elections for a Grand Constituent Assembly within eight months from the date of signature of this Accord.

c. The duly elected Grand Constituent Assembly will formulate a Constitution under which general elections for the President and the Parliament will be held within the prescribed period of 18 months mentioned above.

iv. A Defence Council comprising two members from each party will be set up to;

a.. enable the formation of a national army.

b. take possession of heavy weapons from all parties and source which may be removed from Kabul and other cities and kept out of range to ensure the security of the Capital.

c. ensure that all roads in Afghanistan are kept open for normal use.

d. ensure that State funds will not be used to finance private armies or armed retainers.

e. ensure that operational control of the armed forces will remain with the Defence Council.

v. There will be an immediate and unconditional release of all Afghan detainees held by the Government and other parties during the armed hostilities.

vi. All public and private buildings, residential areas and properties occupied by different armed groups during the hostilities shall be returned to their original owners. Effective steps shall be taken to facilitate the return of displaced persons to their respective homes and locations.

vii. An All-Party Committee will be constituted to supervise control over the monetary system and currency regulations will be brought into effect to keep it them conformity with existing Afghan banking laws and regulations.

viii. A Committee will be constituted to supervise the distribution of food, fuel and essential commodities in Kabul city.

ix. A cease-fire will come into force with immediate effect. After the formation of the Cabinet, there should be a permanent cessation of hostilities.

x. A Joint Commission comprising representatives of the OIC and of all Afghan Parties will be formed to monitor the cease-fire and cessation of hostilities.

In confirmation of the above Accord, the following have affixed their signatures hereunder, on Sunday, March 7th 1993 in Islamabad, Pakistan.

Professor Burhanuddin Rabbani — Jamiate-e-Islami:

President of the Islamic State of Afghanistan

Maulvi Muhammad Nabi Mohammadi — Harakat-e-Inqilab-e-Islami.
Pir Syed Ahmed Gilani — Mahaz-e-Milli.
Sheikh Asif Mohseni — Harakat-e-Islami.
Engineer Gulbuddin Hekmatyar — Hizb-e-Islami.
Professor Sibghatullah Mujaddedi — Jabha-e-Nijat-e-Milli
Engineer Ahmed Shah Ahmedzai — Ittehad-e-Islami.
Ayatullah Fazil — Hizb-e-Wahdat-e-Islami.

There are some major factors that immediately affect the process of power-sharing in Afghanistan. These are:

I. Underdevelopment — This challenge threatens all aspects of life with destruction and leads to all sorts of corruption.

II. The Geopolitical Ethnic Problems:

This problem, as shown in figure 3, threatens the very integrity of Afghanistan. The Pukhtoon or Pushtoon who constitute around 43% are concentrated mainly in the south, east and west of Afghanistan and they have other related Pushtoon tribes in the NWFP in Pakistan. In the north there are Tajiks(24%) and Uzbecks (6%.). In the Islamic perspective, there are some principles that should do away with such ethnicity but unless people are really committed Muslims, mottoes will continue to be slogans and values are mere words.

Many Uzbeck ethnic groups at present help Rashid Dostum who has been involved in PDPA since 1986, and who, due to many differences among PDPA members and factions turned to Ahmed Shah Masood and both managed to control Mazar-e-Sharif, the second largest city in the north of Afghanistan. A war erupted between the two leaders in which Ahmed Shah Masood pushed Dostum out of the centre of Kabul City, causing many casualties..

III. The Sectarian Problem: There are many sects in Afghanistan, the most important of which are Sunni (85%), and Shi'ite (8-10%), followed by Ismaili, Sikh and other sectarian groups. The most dangerous rift is the Sunni-Shia conflict which finds support abroad,

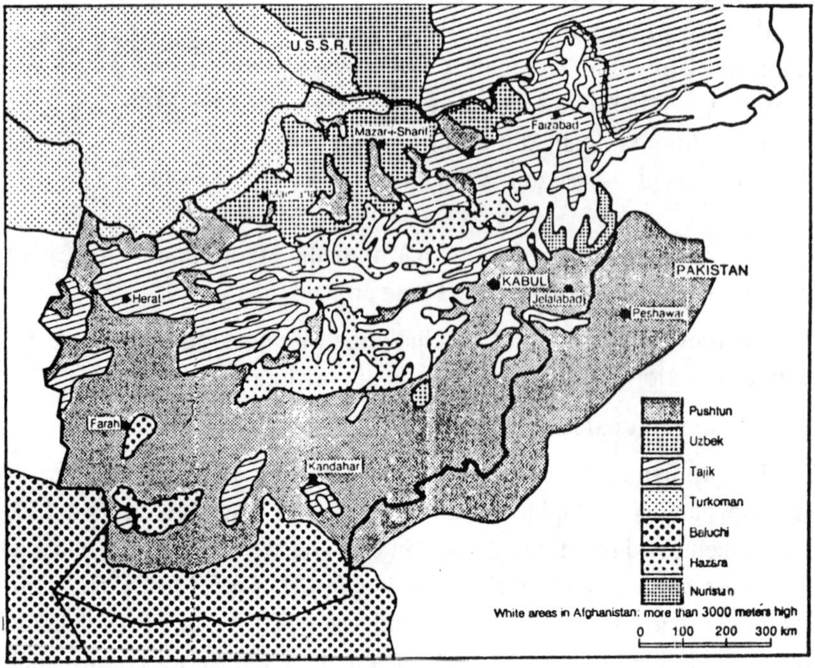

Fig. 3

IV. The Heavy Weapons: The people of Afghanistan are well-armed and the various different parties possess heavy weapons, especially the Jamiat-e-Islami, the Hizb-e-Islami, the Hizb-e-Wahdat (the Shi'ite) and recently the Militia of General Dostum. These parties have means of getting arms if they do not receive them free. Removing arms from Kabul will require a comprehensive plan specifying types and amounts of arms to be removed, the distance they should be stored from Kabul, and a definite timescale for the operation.

operation.

V. The Distrust Among Different Leaders: This is one of the main causes of many of the other problems. The problem of the Ministry of Defence is actually a problem of lack of trust and sheer rivalry and competition between Hekmatyar and Ahmed Shah Masood. Ahmed Shah Masood was the first leader to enter and conquer Kabul in spite of the fact that Hekmatyar's men had been stationed around Kabul for many years waiting for this great opportunity. Some of them had managed to enter Kabul earlier but were pushed out by Masood's or Dostum's forces. There are many differing views on this issue. Hekmatyar himself says Dostum's men pushed his forces out of Kabul.

The recent history of the conflict shows that many power-sharing attempts were introduced, but all of them failed due to rejection by the powerful Mujahideen parties and their firm refusal to agree to a cease-fire until the Communists were removed. The following illustrate some of the attempts at power-sharing:

The National Fatherland Front: established by Babrak Karmal on December 29th 1980 aiming at winning over all liberal and progressive forces. This failed to gain the trust of the people.

The National Reconciliation Programme: established by Najibullah in 1987. Its second paragraph said that the regime was prepared to share power even with those who were against the PDPA government in Kabul. The emphasis was on sharing power, but the Mujahideen insisted that full power be handed over to them.

The Diego Cordovez attempt to establish a national government of peace and reconstruction in July 1988 after the Geneva Accord was signed.

The Russian Peace Offensive: established by Yuli Voronstov and Eduard Shevardnadze in 1988-89, trying to create a broad-based government in Afghanistan in which power is shared by Mujahideen with Muslims from the Communist regime in Kabul. It was known as the ten point programme.

The Second Afghan Interim Government (AIG): was formed in February 1989 and presided over by Mujaddedi as President and Sayyaf as Prime Minister. It dissolved after one year on 15th. February 1990. Only four countries recognised the AIG — Saudi Arabia, Sudan, Malaysia and Bahrain.

Future Trends

In view of the prevailing situation and in view of the Islamabad Accord, Afghanistan might remain split into multiple centres of power with a loose central authority. The cease-fire may continue for quite some time, but the civil war is not expected to come to a final end in the near future.

The conflict will continue between the Mujahideen and the secularists, and also amongst the powerful armed parties of the Mujahideen themselves until they become truly political parties. The second generation of leaders might be luckier than the first generation leaders. They are more in the habit of dialogue, and there is more mutual respect and trust between them, which might make them able to deal peacefully with one another and establish a stable community based on power-sharing.

Many observers are happier with the Islamabad Accord than with previous agreements.They see major differences in the Accord that might lead to its success. These are:

It is an improvement on the Peshawar Accord of 24th April1992 on several scores.

1. Iran has agreed to support the Islamabad Accord.
2. The two Shi'ite parties have agreed on the Accord, but this prevented Maulvi Younas Khalis (Hizb Islami) from participating in the present government under formation.
3. The powers of both the President and Prime Minister were defined to a great extent, but some loose terms like 'consultation' or 'proper distance' need further clarification.
4. It set a timeframe for formation of the Cabinet, but this is hard to implement. The implementation of the Accord and formation of the

Cabinet need more detailed discussion.
5. It stipulated the programme for the handing over of heavy weapons to the government, but the most suitable distance for storage of these weapons is still negotiable.
6. It set some guidelines for establishing justice, such as the return of public and private properties to their original owners and the relocation of displaced people.

In spite of these optimistic views, we see that the Afghanistan system of power-sharing may need years to become properly established and to satisfy the people and the different political parties.

The main key figures in possible future conflicts over power in Afghanistan are:

1. Engineer Gulbuddin Hikmatyar
2. Professor Burhanuddin Rabbani
3. Professor Abdu Rab Rasool Sayyaf
4. Engineer Ahmed Shah Masoud
5. Mawlawi Mohammad Ismael Khan (Herat)
6. The Shite groups (especially the Wahdat Party)
7. The Militia leader — Abdul Rasheed Dostum
8. The Islamic Movement (the second generation)
9. The secularist and Western-oriented powers

Unless all these leaders and factions come to understand the social and power change that is needed in Afghanistan, the future conflict could still be the bloodiest in the history of Afghanistan.

NOTES

1. Arnold, Anthony — 'Afghanistan, The Soviet Invasion in Perspective'. Hoover Institution Press; Stanford University, Stanford, California, USA.

2. Bush, George —' National Security Strategy of the United States'; 1991-1992. Brassy's (US) Inc. A Macmillan Publishing Company; New York.

3. Colonel (Retd). Ahmad N.D. — 'The Survival of Afghanistan.' Institute of Islamic Culture; Lahore, Pakistan.

4. Dupree, Louis — 'Afghanistan.' Princeton University Press; Princeton, New Jersey, USA.

5. El-Helbawy, Kamal — 'International Strategies in the Afghan Issue' (Arabic).

6. El-Helbawy, Kamal —' How to understand Afghanistan,' (Arabic)

7. Lt. General (Retd) Matinuddin, Kamal — 'Power Struggle in the Hindu Kush'. Wajidalis; Lahore, Pakistan.

8. Roy, Olivier — 'Islam and Resistance in Afghanistan.' Cambridge University Press; Cambridge, United Kingdom.

THE FUTURE OF POWER-SHARING IN EGYPT

Dr. Essam Al-Erian

Introduction:

Following the July 1952 Revolution, the Egyptian political arena witnessed a transformation from a loose parliamentary system to a single party regime that outlawed all political parties and harshly repressed any opposition. Inititally, the revolution - thanks to its nationalist libertarian slogans - succeeded in gaining the sympathy and support of a large sector of the population, including the major Islamic group, the Muslim Brotherhood, who participated in the revolution and was initially excepted from the general ban imposed on political parties. Intense competition marked the relationship amongst the members of the Revolution Command Council which resorted to tyrannical repressive measures to tighten its grip on the country.

The policies adopted in the economic sector caused the majority of the population to suffer and burdened the state with huge debts. Prior to the revolution, Britain - which occupied Egypt for more than seventy years - owed Egypt around £500 million, and the Egyptian pound was equivalent to slightly more than one pound Sterling or more than 2.5 U.S. dollars. Today, Egypt's non-military foreign debts alone amount to $40 billion and the Egyptian pound is equivalent to no more than a third of a dollar.

The role of the Islamists in the political arena became, once again, more visible following the death of President Nasir and the accession to power of President Sadat. In the meantime, the competition amongst the various centres of power in the regime intensified, only to be met by two new forms of challenge: Islamic revival and popular discontent.

The Components of Power:

Despite the discontinuation of pluralistic democracy soon after the 1952 coup, power continued to be divided - at least in theory - into the executive and the legislative. The executive consisted of the 'Presidential Establishment' and the 'Council of Ministers'.

The Presidency:

The Presidential Establishment derives its legitimacy from what is known as the popular referendum. It has supreme authority and reserves the right to form the cabinet. According to the tradition implemented after the revolution, the head of state may, hold - in addition to the post of the presidency - the post of prime minister, the post of head of the ruling party and the post of commander in chief of the armed forces . Furthermore, the Presidential Establishment enjoys the right to declare a state of emergency, the right to issue decrees that automatically become laws, and the right to dissolve the People's Assembly.

Unlike the situation that prevailed during Nasir's time, today's Presidential Establishment in Egypt, like its predecessor, has no real political or social base. A base of profiteers is the only support this establishment now enjoys in the civilian sector. It is the military establishment that continues to control the politics of the country through its intimate relationship with the presidency.

The Cabinet:

The Prime Minister is picked by the President, and while the Prime Minister nominates prospective cabinet members, the final endorsement and appointment lies in the hands of the President himself. The nomination and susbsequent appointment is done on personal basis, and members of the cabinet do not usually represent political parties. In most cases they are individuals who fit a certain set of criteria tailored to suit the trend adopted by the Presidential Establishment, and usually are technocrats or come from the business sector.

The Legislature:

This consists of the People's Assembly and the Shura (consultative) Council. The People's Assembly is now completely controlled by the ruling National Party which was previously known as the Arab Socialist Union. The Shura Council lacks real authority and has no powers whatsoever. The population on the whole has no respect for this establishment which fails to represent the demands or the aspirations of the Egyptian people.

Nominations to the People's Assembly are subject to the scrutiny and approval of the Executive Authority (the Presidency and the Cabinet). Nominees are mostly civil servants who depend on the government for living. Despite the alleged pluralism, the country continues to be run by single party politics.

The Judiciary:

The Presidential Establishment has tried many times, unsuccessfully, to subjugate the Judiciary to government policies. There are still many, judges and lawyers, who insist on adhering to the ethics and norms of the legal practice. Recently, Judge Tariq Al-Bishri issued a verdict which nullified a presidential decree referring some civilian defendents to martial courts. Similarly, on 19 May 1990, the Supreme Constitutional Court ruled that the People's Assembly elected in 1987 was unconstitutional, ordered its dissolution and called for new elections. Instead of implementing the Court's ruling, the President issued a Republican Decree on 26 September ordering the suspension of the Assembly and authorising a popular referendum on its dissolution in October 1990.

The Opposition:

The opposition is widely spread through popular and vocational sectors with varying ideological, cultural and intellectual commitments. The most prominent groups in the opposition are: the Muslim Brotherhood, Al-Wafd Party, the Labour Socialist Party, At-Tajammu' party and Al-Ahrar Party.

Due to the military dictatorship and political despotism of the present regime policies on the local, regional and international levels have been most injurious to the stability and prosperity of the country. On the one hand, the democratic process has - after constantly resorting to the method of falsifying the elections - been completely suspended, while on the other hand local and regional 'threats' are being invented by the regime in order to justify its despotic nature and to prolong the suspension of pluralistic democracy.

The opposition in Egypt has always had a set of essential demands. These include:

1) The resumption of the democratic process through free parliamentary elections to the People's Assembly.

2) Insuring the independent supervision of elections - as stated by the constitution - by the Judiciary, and the non-intervention in these elections of the executive establishment or any of its affiliated departments or officials, especially the Presidency, the interior ministry and the provincial administrations. Precautionary measures should be taken in order to prevent vote-rigging and the coercion, threatening or bribing of citizens.

3) An end to the declared state of emergency and martial law.

4) The abrogation of the laws on terrorism. These laws have only been used against the political opposition to the regime, and particularly against the Islamic Movement.

5) The relinquishment of the National Party by the President whose powers should be limited in order to guarantee non-intervention in the legislative and judiciary establishments.

6) The adoption of the principle of power rotation and power-sharing

among political parties.

7) Liberating the press and media from government control, and providing equal opportunities in the official press for all political parties.

8) Providing the People's Assembly with real powers including the power to dismiss the cabinet, to legislate or abrogate laws, and to modify or amend the budget.

9) Reforming the election law and withdrawing the President's right to appoint a number of the members of the People's Assembly.

The Islamic Experience:

Egyptian President Hosni Mubarak was quoted as saying that he had learned a lesson from the experience of Algeria. He declared many times that he would not repeat the same mistake of granting the Islamists the right to officially engage in political activities or participate in democratic elections. So far, the Muslim Brotherhood, the largest Islamic group in Egypt, continues to be prevented from acting as a political party or officially forming one.

The law in Egypt has always prevented 'religious' groups from practising politics, and that is why in the past the Muslim Brotherhood resorted to nominating a number of their candidates to the parliamentary elections by joining the list of an officially registered political party.

In principle, the Muslim Brotherhood have always believed in the viability of the parliamentary system. The founder of the group, Imam Hassan Al-Banna, nominated himself - together with a number of other Brotherhood members - twice: in 1942 and in 1945. Talking about the role of Parliament, Imam Al-Banna said: "The Parliament should not be restricted only to the leaders of political parties; it should act as a platform for the entire nation where every good idea or constructive suggestion is announced and where the desires and aspirations of the nation are expressed."

Through most of President Nasir's rule (1952-1970), the Muslim

Brotherhood were outlawed, their leaders and suspected members or sympathisers executed or detained and their image savagely distorted by the official media. Throughout the seventies, the Muslim Brotherhood worked hard in order to re-establish themselves in the community amid a sweeping wave of Islamic revival. As their political influence grew, President Sadat decided to crack down on them, ordering the confiscation of their offices, the closure of their newspaper and the detention of their leader Omar At-Tilmisani and many of his followers in September 1981.

The Muslim Brotherhood had two recent Parliamentary experiences; the first in 1984 when they entered into a political alliance with Al-Wafd Party, and the second in 1987 when they made an alliance with the Labour Socialist Party. The latter officially adopted Islam as a motto in its annual conference in 1989, and has since been strongly allied in political activity with the Muslim Brotherhood.

In the 1990 elections, most of the political parties and groups in Egypt (including Al-Wafd, Al-Ahrar and the Brotherhood-Labour Party alliance) boycotted the elections to protest against the overt intervention and manipulation of the process by the government.

The Political Agenda:

The Brotherhood's parliamentary candidates introduced themselves to the Egyptian people as advocates of an Islam-based reform. They introduced the slogan "ISLAM IS THE SOLUTION" implying that the main problems suffered nowadays by Egyptian society can be resolved gradually if the Islamic way of life were to be reinstated and the Islamic Shari'ah Laws were implemented. The Brotherhood's political agenda included the following:

1) The government must grant citizens their civil rights and embark on a serious and sincere transition to an Islamic form of democracy in which the nation is the source of legitimacy and the Qur'an and the Sunnah (traditions of the Prophet) are the sources of legislation.

2) Proper education is the means to prepare a strong and faithful

generation capable of meeting the challenges facing the Egyptian people. Educational programmes should be based on Islam and the Arab culture.

3) The information and media policies should also be based on Islamic values in order to serve as constructive rather than destructive tools in the quest for rebuilding the Arab-Islamic civilization.

4) The economic problems of the nation will only find a resolution if Islamic economic principles are applied. These include an immediate stop to favoritism, exploitation and corruption; the abolition of the western style interest-based banking system and its replacement with the Islamic banking transactions that guarantee fairness and equality and close all avenues leading to monopoly and injustice; and the collection of *zakat* from the rich and distributing it among the poor.

5) Irrespective of foreign pressures and the decisions adopted by the major powers of the world, Islamic questions such as those of Palestine, Keshmir, Bosnia, etc. must be supported and defended in all possible ways.

6) The objective of an Islamic opposition is to pressure the government to implement Islamic Law and to respect the collective rights of the nation as well as the basic rights of individual citizens. The objective of such an Islamic opposition is not merely to compete for power.

However, in spite of the peaceful and civilised approach of the Muslim Brotherhood, their declared commitment to true and real democracy and their belief in pluralism and power-sharing, the movement has been prevented from pursuing its objectives. An example of this is that the Labour party with whom the Muslim Brotherhood have an alliance is frequently threatened by the government, who would like to ban it for no other reason than cooperating with the Muslim Brotherhood. In addition, the only Egyptian newspaper the Brotherhood have access to - Ash-Sha'b, which is published twice weekly - is threatened with closure by the authorities.

Unions and Syndicates:

Traditionally, the Muslim Brotherhood and other smaller Islamic groups have targeted trade unions and syndicates as platforms for their cultural and social activities and for expressing Islamic ideas. The Muslim Brotherhood have been doing very well in most of these unions, gaining overwhelming successes which showed the popular support enjoyed by the Movement. These unions and syndicates include:

- the Syndicate of Doctors
- the Syndicate of Pharmacists
- the Syndicate of Engineers
- the Syndicate of Lawyers
- the Syndicate of Teachers
- the Associations of University Professors
- Student Unions at the Egyptian universities
- Islamic Relief Organisations.

Alarmed by the victory achieved by all 16 Muslim Brotherhood candidates in the recent election of the Lawyers Syndicate (out of a total of 25 seats), the Government - supported in this by secular elements - formulated a new law to curb the growing influence of the Islamists. According to the new law, the election results for any syndicate or union will only be recognised if more than 50% of the syndicate members cast the ballot in the first round or 33% in the second round. If this condition is not fulfilled, the law states that the Government would appoint a council to run the syndicate.

This law, which the Government claims is aimed at preserving democracy, is nothing but a stab in the back of democracy. Can one really force the people to go to the ballot boxes? One can only try to persuade them. What happens if only 30% or 32% of the members of a certain syndicate cast the ballot? According to this law, the elections are null and democracy is out. Who then can guarantee - in view of the authorities' intervention and imposed scrutiny - that the real number of voters is not manipulated? We have here a clear case of a conspiracy against democracy and against the right of the people to choose and express their opinions.

The Phenomenon of Radicalism:

While the Muslim Brotherhood maintain a solid position in opposing radicalism, aggression and violence of all kinds, they believe that the Egyptian regime is responsible for the regrettable wave of terrorism that is currently sweeping through Egyptian society. Much of this violence stems from the frustration and provocation resulting from repressive, corrupt and unjust government policies and measures. The young men who are involved in such radical activities could have been contained and tamed through a genuine democratic process in which their grievances and complaints would have found their way to settlement and resolution, and as a result violence would gradually fade out and eventually disappear.

Not only has the regime been driving the youth towards more and more radicalisation and the use of violence, but it has also been making up stories about alleged foreign threats, conspiracies and intervention attempts, trying to link many innocent individuals and groups inside Egypt with foreign countries or organisations. The only reason one can think of for these unwise actions on the part of the authorities in Egypt is their certain desire to conceal true facts and to convince the world that the harsh repressive measures and the repeated violations of human rights are justified.

It is also regrettable that Western democracies have been partly responsible for the Egyptian crisis. The constant support and aid received by dictatorships and despotic governments from the West encourages them to escalate their onslaught on human rights and to turn a deaf ear to the calls for reform and democratisation.

Is there a future?

At present the future looks gloomy. The regime does not seem to have a strategy for resolving the current crisis in Egypt. The hostile position taken by the regime against Islamic activists only widens the rift between the regime and the nation which is becoming increasingly supportive of and sympathetic to the Islamic Movement. There is no doubt that dictators in general fear democracy and consider it to be the worst option as far as their status is concerned. The Egyptian regime in particular is anxious not to allow what happened in Algeria to be repeated in Egypt. But for how long can the pressure be controlled and the popular anger restrained?

No matter what the regime tries to do, there is only one solution to the crisis and only one way to a better future, and that is true and real democracy.

APPENDICES

THE CONTRIBUTORS
Brief Biographies

Professor John Keane is a Professor of Politics at the University of Westminster and Director of the Centre for the Study of Democracy. He was educated at the Universities of Adelaide, Toronto and Cambridge. He is the author of *Public Life and Late Capitalism* (1984); *Democracy and Civil Society* (1988) and *The Media and Democracy* (1991). His biography of Thomas Paine is forthcoming. He is a contributor to leading journals including the *International Social Science Journal*, *Political Studies* and the *Times Literary Supplement*. He was a senior visiting fellow at the European University Institute in Florence in 1990; and during 1991 he was visiting professor at the Central European University in Prague. He was elected a Fellow of the Royal Society of Arts in 1992.

Professor Ernes Gellner is William Wyse Professor of Anthorpology at the University of Cambridge. . He is an internationally recognised philospopher and sociologist. He is a regular contributor to the *Times Litrerary Supplement* and is a visiting Professor at the Central European University in Prague. He is author of many articles and books, including: *Arabs and Berbers* (1972), *Contemporary Thought and Politics* (1974), *Legitimation of Belief* (1974), *Muslim Society* (1981), *Nations and Nationalism* (1983), *State and Society in Soviet Thought* (1988), *Plough, Sword and Book: the Structure of Human Society* (1988) and *Postmodernism, Reason and Religion* (1992).

Francois Burgat is a Senior Researcher at the French National Centre for Scientific Research (CNRS) based in Cairo, Egypt, at the Centre d'études et de documentation jurisdique, économique et sociale (CEDEJ). Mr. Burgat who, in addition to his French mother tongue, masters both English and Arabic worked as an Assistant Professor at the Faculty of Law, the University of Constantine in Algeria from 1973 to 1980. From September 1980 to June 1982 he worked as an Assistant Professor at the Institut d'études politiques, the University of Grenoble. He is the author of *Les Villages socialistes de la révolution agrire* (1984), *L'Islamisme au Maghreb: la voix du Sud* (1988), and its Arabic version *Al Islam Al Siyassi: Sawt Al-Jenoub* (1992). His book *The Islamic Movement in the North of Africa* is forthcoming in English.

Rachid Al-Ghannouchi is the leader of the Tunisian opposition An-Nahdah (renaissance) Party. He was working on his Ph.D. thesis titled 'Public Liberties in the Islamic State' when he was forced into exile. He was jailed for varying terms during President Bourguiba's era and in 1987 he was given a life imprisonment sentence which the authorities appealed against and ordered a retrial which ended with death sentences for him and three of his followers. He was forced into exile by the present regime after his party was outlawed and thousands of his followers killed, jailed or banished. He is considered to be among the most prominent contemporary Islamic political thinkers and has so far published several books (all in Arabic) including: *We and the West*, *Our Way to Civilization*,*The Islamic Movement and Modernisation*, *The Woman Between the Qur'an and Society*, *The Basic Principles of Democracy and Islamic Government*, *The Rights of Citizens in the Islamic State*, *Destiny and Man in ibn Taymiya's Thought*, and *The Rights of Non-Muslims in the Islamic State* (this last book is available in English). His book Public Liberties in the Islamic Political System (which was the proposed theme of his Ph.D.) is forthcoming.

Dr. Mohamed Salim El-Awa is a Professor of Comparative Law and an attorney at the Court of Cassation in Egypt. He obtained his Ph.D. in Law from the University of London in 1972. He has contributed many articles to local and international periodicals and has written several books including: *The Origins of Islamic Criminal System* (1983) *Copts and Islam* (1987), , *The Political System of the Muslim State* (1989), *Punishment in the Islamic Law* (1989) and *Constitutional and Political Crises in Egypt 1987-1990* (1991).

Dr. Hassan Al-Alkim is an Associate Professor of Political Science at the University of the United Arab Emirates. He was educated at the Universities of Seattle (U.S.A. where he obtained his B.A. in Political Science) and Exeter (U.K. where he obtained his M.A. and Ph.D.) He is a member of the Editorial Boad of the Arab Journal of Political Science. He is the author of *An-Nizam As-Siyasi Al-Islami*, *The Foreign Policy of the United Arab Emirates* and *Qadadya Islamiyah Mu'asirah*. His book *The Dynamics of the GCC States' Foreign Policy-Making is forthcoming.*

Dr. Abdallah Al-Akailah is a lecturer of general administration at the Department of Economy and Administration at the Jordanian University. He completed his undergraduate studies at the Jordanian University and obtained his Masters and Ph.D. degrees in general administration from the University of South California (1978-1982). He has been a member of the Jordanian Parliament (1984-1993) and held the post of Education Minister for five months in 1990/1991.

Dr. Nasir Sani is a Member of the Kuwaiti Parliament that was elected in October 1992. In Parliament he sits on the committees for Foreign Affairs and Finance. He was educated in the U.S. where he completed his Masters in Administration and in Birmingham, England, where he completed his Ph.D also in Administration.

Mustafa Ali is a senior member of the Islamic Party of Malaysia (PAS). He is a former Member of Parliament and ex-Deputy Minister of Science and Environment.

Anwar Haddam is a nuclear physicist who until December 1991 lecturered physics at the University of Science and Technology in Algiers. He was among the parliamentary candidates of the Islamic Salvation Front (FIS) who won in the first round of elections held on 26 December 1991. Now he heads the FIS Parliamentary Delegation to Europe and the U.S.A., speaking for FIS parliamentarians.

Rachid Ben Eissa is an Islamic activist from Algeria who is based in Paris where he works for UNESCO. He is a social scientist by training and was associated with the famous Muslim thinker, Malek Ben Nabi. He founded the annual Pensee Islamique conferences that were a notable event in newly independent Algeria. In the past 20 years he has travelled and lectured widely in the Muslim world, providing audiences with an engaging and penetrating analysis of contemporary Islam.

Kamal El-Helbawy is Advisor and Editor in Chief at the Arabic Section of the Institute of Policy Studies in Islamabad, Pakistan. He is currently in the final stages of his Ph.D. investigating International Strategies. He translated several books from Arabic to English and from English to Arabic and authored several others including: *Translation and Islamisation*, *Afghanistan: An Attempt to Understand* and *International Strategies over the Afghan Issue*.

Dr. Essam Al-Erian is a medical doctor by profession. He graduated from the Fuculty of Medicine, Cairo University in 1977, completed his Masters degree in Clinical Pathology in 1986 and is currently doing his Ph.D. in Clinical Pathology at the same University. He was one of the founders of the Islamic Students Movement in Egypt in the seventies (known then as the *Al-Jama'ah Al-Islamiyah*) . He is an active member of the Muslim Brotherhood, and has since 1986 been a member of the Doctors Syndicate and is currently its Assistant Secretary General. He was a member of the Egyptian People's Assembly (parliament) from 1987 to 1990.

BIBLIOGRAPHY

Suggested further reading on topics related to Power-sharing Islam

In English

Abu Sulaiman, A. *The Islamic Theory in International Relations.* Wshington, 1981

Asad, M. *State and Government in Islam.* Gibraltar, 1985

Asad, M. *Islam at the Crossroads.* Gibraltar, 1982

Asad, M. *The Road to Mecca.* Gibraltar, 1981

Cleveland, W. *Islam Against the West: Shakib Arslan and the Campaign for Islamic Nationalism.* Austin, 1985

Dabashi, H. *Authority in Islam: from the rise of Muhammad to the Establishment of the Umayyads.* New Brunswick, 1989.

Daniel, N. *Islam and the West: The Making of an Image.* Edinburgh, 1960.

Daniel, N. *Islam, Europe and Empire.* Edinburgh, 1966.

El-Affendi, A. *Who Needs an Islamic State?* London 1991.

Enayat, Hamid. *Modern Islamic Political Thought.* 1991

Esposito, J. *The Islamic Threat: Myth or Reality.* Oxform Un. 1992

Gellner, E. *Muslim Society.* 1981

Ibn Khaldoun, *The Muqaddimah: An Introduction to History* (Translated by Franz Rosenthal), Princeton Univ. Press, 1967.

Ibn Taymiyah: *On Public and Private Law in Islam*, trans. O. Farrukh, Beirut: Khayat's, 1966.

Kedourie, E. *Democracy and Arab Political Culture*. Washington, 1992.

Kerr, M. *Islamic Reform: the Legal and Political Theories of Muhammad Abduh and Rashid Rida*. Berkeley and Los Angeles: University of California Press, 1966.

Rodinson, M. *Europe and the Mystique of Islam* (translated by Roger Veinus). London, 1988.

Said, E.W. *Covering Islam*. London, 1981

Sivan, E. *Radical Islam: Medieval Theology and Modern Politics*. Yale, 1985.

Southern, R.W. *Western Views of Islam in the Middle Ages*. Cambridge, 1962.

Vatikiotis, P.J. *Islam and the State*. London, 1987

In French

Bennabi, M. *Vocation de l'Islam*. Paris, 1954

Djaie, H. *L'Europe et l'Islam*. Paris, 1978

Ducellier, A, A. *Le Miroir de l'Islam, Musulmans et Christiens d'Orient au Moyen Âge* . Paris, 1971.

Mawardi: *Les status gouvernementaux*, trans. E. Fagnan. Paris, 1982

In Arabic

Aqqad, M.A. *Ad-Dimuqradiyah Fil Islam.* Cairo, 1971

Arabi, M.A. *Nizam Al-Hukm Al-Islami*. Beirut, 1968

Amarah, M. *Ma'rakat Al-Islam Wa Usul Al-Hukm*. 1989

Ansari, A. *Ash-Shura Wa Atharuha Fid-Dimuqradiyah*, Sidon.

Awa, M.S. *Fi Nizam Al-Hukm Al-Islami.* Cairo, 1989

Bennabi, M. *Al-Qadaya Al-Kubra.* Beirut, 1991

Burgat, Francois. *Al-Islam As-Siyasi: Sawt Al-Janub.* Cairo, 1992

Darwish, Q. Rachid Al-Ghannouchi: Hiwarat. London, 1992

Ghannouchi, R. *Al-Hurriyat Al-'Ammah Fid-Dawlah Al-Islamiyah.* Beirut, (forthcoming)

Hilmi, M. *Nizam Al-Khalifah Fil-Fikr Al-Islami.* Cairo, 1977

Ibn Taymiyah. *As-Siyasah Ash-Shar'iyah Fi Islah Ar-Ra'i War-Ra'iyah.* Beirut, 1969

Kawakibi, A. *Taba'i' Al-Istibdad.* Algiers, 1988

Mawardi, A. *Al-Ahkam As-Sultaniyah.* Beirut 1978

Rayis, D. *An-Nazariyat As-Siyasiyah Al-Islamiyah.*

Shawi, Tawfiq. *Fiqh Ash-Shura Wal Istisharah.* Cairo, 1992

Wafi, Abdulwahid. *Al-Hurriyah Fil Islam.* Cairo, 1986

Zaidan, A. Usul Ad-Da'wah. Baghdad, 1976

Zaidan, A. Al-Madkhal Lidirasat Ash-Shari'ah Al-Islamiyah. Baghdad, 1976

For more references please refer to the notes on pages: 63, 75-76, 88-89 & 158)

GLOSSARY

'Adl: staightness, justice or fairness; the verb is **'adala**: to act justly.

'Aql:sense, reason, mind or rationality. Its root is the verb **'Aqala** which means to hobble (the camel) with the **'Iqal**, a cord used for this purpose.

Bait Al-Mal: treasury or exchequer.

Da'wah: appeal, request or call. **Islamic Da'wah** is the act of calling to Islam, cf. missionary work. The verb is *Da'a*, that is to call, summon or invite.

Dar Al-Harb: **Dar** is house or home and **Harb** is war. It is a term used to describe enemy territory or a country that is under the political authority of a non-Muslim government that is in war with the Muslims.

Deen: religion, creed or faith. The verb is **Dana**, that is to profess. The verb also means to owe someone something.. **Yawm Ad-Deen** is the Day of Judgment

Fiqh: understanding, comprehension or knowledge. It also means Islamic jurisprudence. The verb **Faqiha** means to understand, to comprehend or to have knowledge. A **Faqih** is a legist or jurisprudent or expert of **Fiqh**.

Hajj: pilgrimmage. The verb is **Hajja** .

Halal: that which allowed, permitted or permissible.

Haqiqah: truth, reality or fact.

Haq: truth, correctness, rightness or right.

Haram: forbidden, prohibited or unlawful.

Hijrah: emigration or exodus. In Islamic history it refers to the emigration of Prophet Mohammad and his followers from Mecca to Medina.

Hudud: the plural of **Hadd** which means edge, border or limit. **Hudud-ullah** are the bounds or restrictions that God has placed on man's freedom or action.

Ijma': unanimity or agreement. In Islamic Law it means: consensus of the authorities in a legal question. It is one of the four **Usul** of Islamic Law.

Ijtihad: effort, exertion, endeavor, diligence or individual judgment. In Islamic Law it means independent judgment in a legal or theological question, based on the four **Usul**.

'Ilm: knowledge, learning, cognition, information. The plural **'Ulum** usually refers to science.

Imam: prayers leader or head of a community or state.

Jahiliyah: state of ignorance or pre-Islamic times. The verb **Jahila** means not to know or to be ignorant. It also means to be irrational or to act foolishly.

Jama'ah: group (of people) or community. The root is **Jama'a** which means to collect, unite or join. **Majmu'ah** also means group or band.

Jihad: holy war against the infidels as a religious duty. It also means battle or fight. The root is **Jahada** which means to endeavor, strive or fight.

Jiziah: head tax on free non-Muslims under Muslim rule.

Khawarij: dissidents or rebels. It refers to the oldest religious sect of Islam formed by rebels who rose against the fourth Caliph Ali Ibn Abi Talib. The root is **Kharaja** and **it** means to walk out, leave, deviate or secede.

Kufr: infidelity, blasphemy or ingratitude. The verb is **Kafara**. A **Kafir** is an infidel or an ungrateful person.

Labbaik: here I am! or your service! The root **Labba** means to follow, obey, respond or comply.

Mu'tazilah: a theological school which introduced speculative dogmatism into Islam. The verb **'Azala** means to remove, isolate, withdraw or detach.

Murabaha: means (in Islamic Law) resale with specification of gain or resale with an advance. The root is the word **Rabiha**: to gain, profit or benefit.

Musawat: equivalence, having equal rights or equality before the law.

Muwajaha Bil-Quwwah: forceful or violent confrontation.

Muwajaha Silmiyah: peaceful confrontation.

Naql: carriage, transport, transportation, removal, transmission, transcription, etc. In Islamic terminology it means tradition.

Qiyas: measure, reference comparison, analogy or deduction by analogy. One of thefour Usul in Islamic Jurisprudence.

Rahmah: mercy, compassion or kindness.

Riddah: apostasy.

Shari'ah or **Shar'**: the Revelation, or the canonical law of Islam.

Shi'ah: followers, adherents or disciples. It is also the name of the faction which recognizes Ali, the Prophet's son-in-law as his rightful successor.

Shura: consultation, deliberation or council.

Taqlid: imitation, copying or blindunquestioning adoption of concepts or ideas. It also means the adoption of the legal decision or opinion of a **Mazhab** or school of jurisprudence.

Tarahum: showing compassion or kindness to one another.

Ummah: nation, people or community.

Usul: assets, principles, fundamentals or rules. In Islamic Law **Usul Al-Fiqh** refers to the four foundations of Islamic Jurisprudence, i.e. the Holy Qur'an, Sunna (traditions of the Prophet), Qiyas (analogy) and Ijma' (consensus). The singular **Asl** also means origin.

Wajib: duty, imperative or obligatory.

Zakat: purity or vindication. In Islamic Law it refers to alms-giving, alms tax or charity.

INDEX